THE PANIZZI LECTURES
1985

Bibliography and
the sociology of texts
D. F. McKENZIE

THE BRITISH LIBRARY

© 1986 D. F. McKenzie

Published by The British Library
Great Russell Street, London WC1B 3DG

British Library Cataloguing in Publication Data
McKenzie, D. F.
  Bibliography and the sociology of texts.
  —— (The Panizzi Lectures; 1985)
  1. Bibliography, Critical
  I. Title II. British Library III. Series
  010'.42 Z1001

ISBN 07123 0085 6

Designed by John Mitchell
Typeset in Linotron Bembo
by Bexhill Phototypesetters, Bexhill-on-Sea
Printed in England
by BAS Printers, Over Wallop

For
Stuart Johnston

Preface

by Lord Quinton
Chairman, British Library Board

The Panizzi Lectures were founded in 1984 as a result of an anonymous donation for the purpose. This generous and imaginative project celebrates the most notable of the librarians of Victorian England, indeed of the whole world in the Nineteenth Century, the effective creator of the British Museum Library at Bloomsbury, which, under a new name, is still today the scholarly heart of the British Library. Sir Anthony Panizzi (1797–1879) became principal librarian in 1856 and in the ensuing decade transformed, by his energy and determination, a comparatively somnolent, if magnificently rich, collection of books into the world's greatest library. By initiating a general catalogue and making collections readily accessible to readers he defined the modern conception of a national research library.

The intention is that each series of Panizzi Lectures should be based on original research and should be concerned with bibliography in the most inclusive sense of the word, ranging from history and literary criticism by way of typography to the physical constitution of written and printed matter, embracing manuscripts, music and maps as well as books in a narrower sense, and reaching out to take in the social and commercial circumstances of their publication. The lectures will, it is hoped, derive much of their material from the British Library's collections.

The first series of these lectures was delivered in late November and early December 1985 by Donald McKenzie, professor of English at Victoria University, Wellington, New Zealand, and about to take up the post of Reader in Textual Criticism at Oxford later in 1986. He has been president of the Bibliographical Society of London and he was for many years a trustee of the National Library of New Zealand. Those fortunate enough to have heard the lectures delivered will be glad to have a direct record of a delightful experience of intellectual vitality.

Foreword

These lectures were conceived and prepared, not as a text destined for print, but as lecture occasions. The challenge, as I saw it, was to sketch an extended role for bibliography at a time when traditional book forms must share with many new media their prime function of recording and transmitting texts. Professional librarians, under pressure from irresistible social changes, are redefining their discipline to describe, house and access sounds, static and moving images with or without words, and a flow of computer-stored information. By contrast, academic bibliography has not as yet found fresh stimulus in those developments, nor tapped the new experience and interests of students for whom books represent only one form of text.

There were two other considerations which it seemed timely to voice. First, although bibliographers have always found interest not only in books themselves but in the social and technical circumstances of text production, it is only recently that historical bibliography (as distinct from descriptive and analytical bibliography and stemmatics) has gained acceptance as a field of study. The partial but significant shift it signals is one from questions of authorial intention and textual authority to those of dissemination and readership as matters of economic and political motive and of the interaction of text and society as an important source of cultural history.

Second, bibliography and textual criticism have for the past 60 years or so normally formed part of a training for scholarly research in literary history. They remain indispensable tools, but literary history and scholarship no longer look quite as they did. Definitive editions have come to seem an impossible ideal in the face of so much evidence of authorial revision and, therefore, of textual instability. Each version has some claim to be edited in its own right, with a proper respect for its historicity as an artefact; and yet the variety of authorized forms has opened up editorial choice in new ways, even to the point of creating, through conflation, quite new versions thought more appropriate to the needs of newly defined markets. Redirecting bibliographical inquiry in a fruitful response to recent developments in critical theory and practice is not easy, and in the succeeding text it is the challenge least adequately met. But my purpose was to express a need and to stimulate discussion. In that sense, I should like to think that it does homage to the spirit of Anthony Panizzi.

Among the many to whom I owe thanks for their support and advice, cautionary and corrective, I mention in particular Albert Braunmuller, Tom Davis, Mirjam Foot, Linda Hardy, John Kidd, Harold Love, David and Rosamond McKitterick, David Norton, Brian Opie, Sarah Tyacke and Ian Willison. Finally, to the trustees of the Panizzi Lectures trust, I can only express my gratitude for the compliment of their invitation and my hope that, at least in some small measure, their expectations and those of the donor were fulfilled.

D.F.M.

The book as an expressive form

My purpose in these lectures – one I hope that might be thought fitting for an inaugural occasion – is simply to consider anew what bibliography is and how it relates to other disciplines. To begin that inquiry, I should like to recall a classic statement by the late Sir Walter Greg. It is this: 'what the bibliographer is concerned with is pieces of paper or parchment covered with certain written or printed signs. With these signs he is concerned merely as arbitrary marks; their meaning is no business of his'.[1] This definition of bibliography, or at least of 'pure' bibliography, is still widely accepted, and it remains in essence the basis of any claim that the procedures of bibliography are scientific.

A recent study by Mr Ross Atkinson supports that view by drawing on the work of the American semiotician, C. S. Peirce.[2] It can be argued, for example, that the signs in a book, as a bibliographer must read them, are simply iconic or indexical. Briefly, iconic signs are those which involve similarity; they represent an object, much as a portrait represents the sitter. In enumerative bibliography, and, even more so in descriptive, the entries are iconic. They represent the object they describe. Textual bibliography, too, may be said to be iconic because it seeks, as Mr Atkinson puts it, 'to reproduce the Object with maximum precision in every detail'. In that way, enumerative,

I

descriptive, and textual bibliography may be said to constitute a class of three *referential* sign systems. Analytical bibliography, however, would form a distinct class of indexical signs. Their significance lies only in the physical differences between them as an index to the ways in which a particular document came physically to be what it is. It is their *causal* status that, in Peirce's terms, makes the signs *indexical*. In the words of Professor Bowers, writing of analytical bibliography, the physical features of a book are 'significant in the order and manner of their shapes but indifferent in symbolic meaning'.[3]

I must say at once that this account comes closer than any other I know to justifying Greg's definition of the discipline. I am also convinced, however, that the premise informing Greg's classic statement, and therefore this refinement of it, is no longer adequate as a definition of what bibliography is and does.

In an attempt to escape the embarrassment of such a strict definition, it is often said that bibliography is not a subject at all but only, as Mr G. Thomas Tanselle once put it, 'a related group of subjects that happen to be commonly referred to by the same term'.[4] Professor Bowers virtually concedes as much in dividing it into enumerative or systematic bibliography, and descriptive, analytical, textual, and historical bibliography.[5] The purity of the discipline which Greg aspired to is to that extent qualified by its particular applications and these in turn imply that the definition does not fully serve its uses.

The problem is, I think, that the moment we are required to explain signs in a book, as distinct from describing or copying them, they assume a symbolic status. If a medium in any sense effects a message, then bibliography cannot exclude from its own proper concerns the relation between form, function and symbolic meaning. If textual bibliography were merely iconic, it could produce only facsimiles of different versions. As for bibliographical analysis, that depends absolutely upon antecedent historical knowledge, for it can only function 'with the assistance of previously gathered information on the techniques of book production'.[6] But the most striking weakness of the definition is precisely its incapacity to accommodate history. Mr Atkinson is quite frank about this. Accepting the bibliographer's presumed lack of concern for the meaning of signs, he writes: 'we are left now only with the problem of historical bibliography'. He cites with approval the comment by Professor Bowers that the numerous fields concerned with the study of printing and its processes both as art and craft are merely 'ancillary to analytical bibliography'.[7] He is therefore obliged to argue that

> historical bibliography is not, properly speaking, bibliography at all. This is because it does not have as its Object material sign systems or documents. Its Object rather consists of certain mechanical techniques and as such it must be considered not part of bibliography but a constituent of such fields as the history of technology or, perhaps, information science.

Such comments, although recent, and indeed advanced in seeking to accommodate bibliography to semiotics as the science of signs, are oddly out of touch with such developments as, for example, the founding of The Center for the Book by the Library of Congress, the American Antiquarian Society's Programme for the History of the Book in American Culture, or proposals for publication of national histories of the book, of which the most notable so far is *L'Histoire de l'Édition Française*.

I am not bold enough to speak of paradigm shifts, but I think I am safe in saying that the vital interests of most of those known to me as bibliographers are no longer fully served by description, or even by editing, but by the historical study of the making and the use of books and other documents. But is it right that in order to accomplish such projects as, for example, a history of the book in Britain, we must cease to be bibliographers and shift to another discipline? It is here, if anywhere, that other disciplines such as history, and especially cultural history, are now making demands of bibliography. Far from accepting that 'historical bibliography is not, properly speaking, bibliography at all', it is tempting to claim, now, that all bibliography, properly speaking, is historical bibliography.

In such a world, Greg's definition of the theoretical basis of bibliography is too limited. As long as we continue to think of it as confined to the study of the non-symbolic functions of signs,

3

the risk it runs is relegation. Rare book rooms will simply become rarer. The politics of survival, if nothing else, require a more comprehensive justification of the discipline's function in promoting new knowledge.

If, by contrast, we were to delineate the field in a merely pragmatic way, take a panoptic view and describe what we severally *do* as bibliographers, we should note, rather, that it is the only discipline which has consistently studied the composition, formal design and transmission of texts by writers, printers, and publishers; their distribution through different communities by wholesalers, retailers, and teachers; their collection and classification by librarians; their meaning for, and – I must add – their creative regeneration by, readers. However we define it, no part of that series of human and institutional interactions is alien to bibliography as we have, traditionally, practised it.

But, like Panizzi himself, faced with everything printed in a world in change, we reach a point where the accretion of subjects, like the collection of books, demands that we also seek a new principle by which to order them. Recent changes in critical theory, subsuming linguistics, semiotics, and the psychology of reading and writing, in information theory and communications studies, in the status of texts and the forms of their transmission, represent a formidable challenge to traditional practice, but they may also, I believe, give to bibliographical principle a quite new centrality.

The principle I wish to suggest as basic is simply this: bibliography is the discipline that studies texts as recorded forms, and the processes of their transmission, including their production and reception. So stated, it will not seem very surprising. What the word 'texts' also allows, however, is the extension of present practice to include all forms of texts, not merely books or Greg's signs on pieces of parchment or paper. It also frankly accepts that bibliographers should be concerned to show that forms effect meaning. Beyond that, it allows us to describe not only the technical but the social processes of their transmission. In those quite specific ways, it accounts for non-book texts, their physical forms, textual versions, technical transmission, institutional control, their perceived meanings, and social effects. It

4

accounts for a history of the book and, indeed, of all printed forms including all textual ephemera as a record of cultural change, whether in mass civilization or minority culture. For any history of the book which excluded study of the social, economic and political motivations of publishing, the reasons why texts were written and read as they were, why they were rewritten and redesigned, or allowed to die, would degenerate into a feebly degressive book list and never rise to a readable history. But such a phrase also accommodates what in recent critical theory is often called text production, and it therefore opens up the application of the discipline to the service of that field too.

In terms of the range of demands now made of it and of the diverse interests of those who think of themselves as bibliographers, it seems to me that it would now be more useful to describe bibliography as the study of the sociology of texts. If the principle which makes it distinct is its concern with texts in some physical form and their transmission, then I can think of no other phrase which so aptly describes its range. Both the word 'texts' and 'sociology', however, demand further comment.

I define 'texts' to include verbal, visual, oral, and numeric data, in the form of maps, prints, and music, of archives of recorded sound, of films, videos, and any computer-stored information, everything in fact from epigraphy to the latest forms of discography. There is no evading the challenge which those new forms have created.

We can find in the origins of the word 'text' itself some support for extending its meaning from manuscripts and print to other forms. It derives, of course, from the Latin *texere*, 'to weave', and therefore refers, not to any specific material as such, but to its woven state, the web or texture of the materials. Indeed, it was not restricted to the weaving of textiles, but might be applied equally well to the interlacing or entwining of any kind of material. The Oxford Latin Dictionary suggests that it is probably cognate with the Vedic 'tāṣṭi', to 'fashion by carpentry', and consequently with the Greek τέκτων and τέχνη.

The shift from fashioning a material medium to a conceptual system, from the weaving of fabrics to the web of words, is also implicit in the Greek ὕφος 'a web or net', from ὑφαίνω 'to

5

weave'. As with the Latin, it is only by virtue of a metaphoric shift that it applies to language, that the verb 'to weave' serves for the verb 'to write', that the web of words becomes a text. In each case, therefore, the primary sense is one which defines a process of material construction. It creates an object, but it is not peculiar to any one substance or any one form. The idea that texts are written records on parchment or paper derives only from the secondary and metaphoric sense that the writing of words is like the weaving of threads.

As much could now be said of many constructions which are not in written form, but for which the same metaphoric shift would be just as proper. Until our own times, the only textual records created in any quantity were manuscripts and books. A slight extension of the principle – it is, I believe, the same principle – to cope with the new kinds of material constructions we have in the form of the non-book texts which now surround, inform, and pleasure us, does not seem to me a radical departure from precedent.

In turning briefly now to comment on the word 'sociology', it is not perhaps impertinent to note that its early history parallels Panizzi's. A neologism coined by Auguste Comte in 1830, the year before Panizzi joined the staff of the British Museum, it made a fleeting appearance in Britain in 1843 in *Blackwood's Magazine,* which referred to 'a new Science, to be called Social Ethics, or Sociology'. Seven years later it was still struggling for admission. *Fraser's Magazine* in 1851 acknowledged its function but derided its name in a reference to 'the new science of sociology, as it is barbarously called'. Only in 1873 did it find a local habitation and a respected name. Herbert Spencer's *The Study of Sociology,* published in that year, provides a succinct description of its role: 'Sociology has to recognize truths of social development, structure and function'.

As I see it, that stress on structure and function is important, although I should resist its abstraction to the point where it lost sight of human agency. At one level, a sociology simply reminds us of the full range of social realities which the medium of print had to serve, from receipt blanks to bibles. But it also directs us to consider the human motives and interactions which texts involve

6

at every stage of their production, transmission and consumption. It alerts us to the roles of institutions, and their own complex structures, in affecting the forms of social discourse, past and present. Those are the realities which bibliographers and textual critics as such have, until very recently, either neglected, or by defining them as strictly non–bibliographical, have felt unable to denominate, logically and coherently, as central to what we do. Historical bibliography, we were told, was not strictly bibliography at all.

A 'sociology of texts', then, contrasts with a bibliography confined to logical inference from printed signs as arbitrary marks on parchment or paper. As I indicated earlier, claims were made for the 'scientific' status of the latter precisely because it worked only from the physical evidence of books themselves. Restricted to the non–symbolic values of the signs, it tried to exclude the distracting complexities of linguistic interpretation and historical explanation.

That orthodox view of bibliography is less compelling, and less surprising, if we note its affinities with other modes of thinking at the time when Greg was writing. These include certain formalist theories of art and literature which were concerned to exclude from the discussion of a work of art any intended or referential meaning. They were current not only in the years when Greg was formulating his definitions, but were still active in the theory of the New Criticism when Professor Fredson Bowers was developing his. The congruence of bibliography and criticism lay precisely in their shared view of the self-sufficient nature of the work of art or text, and in their agreement on the significance of its every verbal detail, however small. In neither case were precedent or subsequent processes thought to be essential to critical or bibliographical practice. The New Criticism showed great ingenuity in discerning patterns in the poem-on-the-page as a self-contained verbal structure. It is not I think altogether fanciful to find a scholarly analogy in analytical bibliography. Compositor studies, for example, have shown a comparable virtuosity in discerning patterns in evidence which is entirely internal, if not wholly fictional.

I shall return to that analogy with the New Criticism, but I am more concerned for the moment to emphasize the point that this confinement of bibliography to non-symbolic meaning, in an attempt to give it some kind of objective or 'scientific' status, has seriously impeded its development as a discipline. By electing to ignore its inevitable dependence upon interpretive structures, it has obscured the role of human agents, and virtually denied the relevance to bibliography of anything we might now understand as a history of the book. Physical bibliography – the study of the signs which constitute texts and the materials on which they are recorded – is of course the starting point. But it cannot define the discipline because it has no adequate means of accounting for the processes, the technical and social dynamics, of transmission and reception, whether by one reader or a whole market of them.

In speaking of bibliography as the sociology of texts, I am not concerned to invent new names but only to draw attention to its actual nature. Derrida's 'Grammatology', the currently fashionable word 'Textuality', the French 'Textologie', or even 'Hyphologie' (a suggestion made, not altogether seriously, by Roland Barthes) would exclude more than we would wish to lose. Nor is bibliography a sub-field of semiotics, precisely because its functions are not merely synchronically descriptive. Our own word, 'Bibliography', will do. It unites us as collectors, editors, librarians, historians, makers and readers of books. It even has a new felicity in its literal meaning of 'the writing out of books', of generating new copies and therefore in time new versions. Its traditional concern with texts as recorded forms, and with the processes of their transmission, should make it hospitably open to new forms. No new names, then; but to conceive of the discipline as a sociology of texts is, I think, both to describe what the bibliography is that we actually do and to allow for its natural evolution.

Nevertheless, I must now turn to consider the special case of printed texts. In doing so, the particular inquiry I wish to pursue is whether or not the material forms of books, the non-verbal elements of the typographic notations within them, the very disposition of space itself, have an expressive function in conveying meaning, and whether or not it is, properly, a bibliographical task to discuss it.

Again, I sense that theory limps behind practice. At one end of the spectrum, we must of course recognize that Erwin Panofsky on perspective as symbolic form has long since made the theme familiar; at the other end, we find that Marshall McLuhan's *Understanding Media* has made it basic to media studies. In our own field, Mr Nicolas Barker, on 'Typography and the Meaning of Words: The Revolution in the Layout of Books in the Eighteenth Century'; Mr David Foxon on Pope's typography; Mr Giles Barber on Voltaire and the typographic presentation of *Candide;* Mr Roger Laufer on 'scripturation' or 'the material emergence of sense' are all distinguished bibliographers demonstrating in one way or another, not the iconic or indexical, but the symbolic function of typographic signs as an interpretive system.[8] Words like the 'articulation' or 'enunciation' of the book in this sense make similar assumptions. Discussions of the morphology of the book in relation to genre or to special classes of readers and markets assume a complex relation of medium to meaning. Journals like *Visible Language* and *Word & Image* were founded specifically to explore these questions. The persistent example of fine printing and the revival of the calligraphic manuscript, and numerous recent studies of the sophisticated displays of text and illumination in medieval manuscript production, also share a basic assumption that forms effect sense.[9]

Perhaps on this occasion the simplest way of exploring some of these issues as they relate to the expressive function of typography in book forms, as they bear on editing, and as they relate to critical theory, is to offer an exemplary case. I have chosen the four lines which serve as epigraph to 'The Intentional Fallacy', the distinguished essay by W. K. Wimsatt Jr. and M. C. Beardsley which was first published in *The Sewanee Review* in 1946.[10] It would, I think, be hard to name another essay which has so influenced critical theory and the teaching of literature in the past forty years. Briefly, they argued that it was pointless to use the concept of an author's intentions in trying to decide what a work of literature might mean, or if it was any good. And of course exactly the same objection must apply, if it holds at all, to the interpretation of a writer's or printer's intentions in presenting a text in a particular form, or a publisher's intentions in issuing it at all.

Let me say at once that my purpose in using an example from this essay is to show that in some cases significantly informative readings may be recovered from typographic signs as well as verbal ones, that these are relevant to editorial decisions about the manner in which one might reproduce a text, and that a reading of such bibliographical signs may seriously shape our judgement of an author's work. I think it is also possible to suggest that their own preconceptions may have led Wimsatt and Beardsley to misread a text, that their misreading may itself have been partly a function of the manner in which it was printed, and that its typographic style was in turn influenced by the culture at large. My argument therefore runs full circle from a defence of authorial meaning, on the grounds that it is in some measure recoverable, to a recognition that, for better or worse, readers inevitably make their own meanings. In other words, each reading is peculiar to its occasion, each can be at least partially recovered from the physical forms of the text, and the differences in readings constitute an informative history. What writers thought they were doing in writing texts, or printers and booksellers in designing and publishing them, or readers in making sense of them are issues which no history of the book can evade.

'The Intentional Fallacy' opens with an epigraph taken from Congreve's prologue to *The Way of the World* (1700). In it, as Wimsatt and Beardsley quote him,

> He owns with toil he wrote the following scenes;
> But, if they're naught, ne'er spare him for his pains:
> Damn him the more; have no commiseration
> For dullness on mature deliberation.
> WILLIAM CONGREVE, Prologue to
> *The Way of the World*

Congreve's authorized version of 1710 reads:

> *He owns, with Toil, he wrought the following*
> *Scenes,*
> *But if they're naught ne'er spare him for his Pains:*
> *Damn him the more; have no Commiseration*
> *For Dulness on mature Deliberation.*

It has not, I think, been observed before that, if we include its epigraph, this famous essay on the interpretation of literature opens with a misquotation in its very first line. Wimsatt and Beardsley say that Congreve 'wrote' the following scenes, but Congreve was a deliberate craftsman. He said he '*wrought*' them. Since the words quoted are ascribed to Congreve, I think we are clearly meant to accept them as his, even if the essay later persuades us that we cannot presume to know what Congreve might have intended them to mean. By adopting that simple change from '*wrought*' to 'wrote', Wimsatt and Beardsley oblige us to make our meaning from their misreading. The epigraph thereby directs us to weaken the emphasis that Congreve placed on his labour of composition: he writes of the '*Pains*' it cost him to hammer out *his* meaning. The changed wording destroys the carefully created internal rhyme, the resonance between what, in the first line, Congreve said he '*wrought*' and, in the second line, its fate in being reduced to '*naught*' by those who misquote, misconstrue, and misjudge him. Congreve's prologue to *The Way of the World* put, in 1700/1710, a point of view exactly opposite to the one which the lines are cited to support.

Less noticeable perhaps are the implications of the way in which the epigraph is printed. For Congreve's precise notation of spelling, punctuation and initial capitals, the 1946 version offers a flat, even insidiously open form. Congreve wrote that '*He owns*' – comma – '*with Toil*' – comma – '*he wrought the following Scenes*'. In their performance of the line, Wimsatt and Beardsley drop the commas. By isolating and emphasizing the phrase, Congreve may be read as affirming his seriousness of purpose, the deliberation of his art. Wimsatt and Beardsley speed past it, their eyes perhaps on a phrase more proper to their purpose in the next line. What their reading emphasizes instead, surrounding it with commas where Congreve had none, is the phrase 'if they're naught'. By that slight change they highlight Congreve's ironic concession that an author's intentions have no power to save him if an audience or reader thinks he is dull. Congreve, without commas, had preferred to skip quickly past that thought. Wimsatt and Beardsley allow us to dwell on it, for in their reading it would seem to justify their rather different argument.

Those shifts of meaning which result from the variants noted are, I believe, serious, however slight the signs which make them. But there are more. In his second couplet, Congreve writes:

> *Damn him the more; have no Commiseration*
> *For Dulness on mature Deliberation.*

Again, it suits the purpose of the epigraph to remove Congreve's irony, but as irony is crucially dependent upon context, the loss is perhaps inevitable. Reading the words literally, Wimsatt and Beardsley must take them to mean: 'If you really think my scenes are dull, don't waste your pity on their author'. But you will note that Congreve gives upper case 'D's for '*Dulness*' and '*Delibera-tion*'. Those personified forms allow two readings to emerge which tell us something of Congreve's experience. The first is that these abstractions have human shapes (they were sitting there in the theatre); the second alludes to the age-old combat between Dulness and Deliberation, or Stupidity and Sense. By reducing all his nouns to lower case and thereby destroying the early eighteenth-century convention, the epigraph kills off Congreve's personified forms, and by muting his irony, it reverses his meaning. Where Congreve's irony contrasts his own '*mature Deliberation*' with the '*Dulness*' of his critics, their meaning has him saying the reader knows best.

If we look again at the form and relation of the words '*Toil*', '*Scenes*' and its rhyme-word '*Pains*', we note that they, too, have initial capitals. The convention thereby gives us in print a visual, semantic and ultimately moral identity between Congreve's own description of his labours ('*Toil . . . Pains*') and their human products who people his plays. The text as printed in the epigraph breaks down those visual links by depriving the words of their capitals. One set of meanings, which stress a writer's presence in his work, is weakened in favour of a preconceived reading which would remove him from it.

Small as it is, this example is so instructive that I should like to explore it further. It bears on the most obvious concerns of textual criticism – getting the right words in the right order; on the semiotics of print and the role of typography in forming meaning;

on the critical theories of authorial intention and reader response; on the relation between the past meanings and present uses of verbal texts. It offers an illustration of the transmission of texts as the creation of the new versions which form, in turn, the new books, the products of later printers, and the stuff of subsequent bibliographical control. These are the primary documents for any history of the book. By reading one form of Congreve's text (1700/1710), we may with some authority affirm certain readings as his. By reading other forms of it (1946), we can chart meanings that later readers made from it under different historical imperatives.

I may believe – as I do – that Wimsatt and Beardsley have mistaken Congreve's meaning; that they have misconceived his relation to his tradition; that they have misreported his attitude to his own audience and readers. At the same time, their misreading has become an historical document in its own right. By speaking to what they perceived in 1946 to be the needs of their own time, not Congreve's in 1700/1710, they have left a record of the taste, thought and values of a critical school which significantly shaped our own choice of books, the way we read them and, in my own case, the way I taught them. The history of material objects as symbolic forms functions, therefore, in two ways. It can falsify certain readings; and it can demonstrate new ones.

To extend that line of argument, I should like to comment briefly on the word '*Scenes*'. We recall first that Congreve's '*Scenes*' cost him '*Pains*'. Next, we should note that his editors and critics have, almost without exception, replaced his meaning of the word with a commoner one of their own. They have defined them by geography and carpentry, as when a scene shifts from a forest to the palace. For Congreve, by contrast, they were neoclassical scenes: not impersonal places in motion, but distinct groups of human beings in conversation. These made up his scenes. For him, it was the intrusion of another human voice, another mind, or its loss, that most changed the scene. The substance of his scenes, therefore, what he '*wrought with Toil*', were men and women. Once we recover that context and follow Congreve's quite literal meaning in that sense, his rhyme of '*Scenes*' with '*Pains*' glows with an even subtler force. What he hints at is a serious critical judgement about all his work: beneath the rippling surface of his comedy there flows a sombre undercurrent of human pain. In a more mundane way, that perception may direct an editor to adopt a typography which divides Congreve's plays into neoclassical scenes, as he himself did in his edition of 1710.

With that last example, it could be argued that we reach the border between bibliography and textual criticism on the one hand and literary criticism and literary history on the other. My own view is that no such border exists. In the pursuit of historical meanings, we move from the most minute feature of the material form of the book to questions of authorial, literary and social context. These all bear in turn on the ways in which texts are then re-read, re-edited, re-designed, re-printed, and re-published. If a history of readings is made possible only by a comparative history of books, it is equally true that a history of books will have no point if it fails to account for the meanings they later come to make.

Though at times they may pretend otherwise, I suspect that few authors, with the kind of investment in their work that Congreve claims, are indifferent to the ways in which their art is presented and received. There is certainly a cruel irony in the fact that Congreve's own text is reshaped and misread to support an argument against himself. Far from offering a licence for his audience and readers to discount the author's meaning, Congreve is putting, with an exasperated irony, the case for the right of authors, as he says in another line of the prologue, 'to assert their Sense' against the taste of the town. When Jeremy Collier wrenched to his own purposes the meaning of Congreve's words, Congreve replied with his *Amendments of Mr Collier's False and Imperfect Citations*. He too had a way with epigraphs and chose for that occasion one from Martial which, translated, reads: 'That book you recite, O Fidentinus, *is* mine. But your vile *re*-citation begins to make it your own'.

With that thought in mind, I should like to pursue one further dimension of the epigraph's meaning which is not in itself a matter of book form. It nevertheless puts Congreve in the tradition of authors who thought about the smallest details of their work as it might be printed, and who directed, collaborated with, or fumed against, their printers and publishers. One such author is Ben Jonson. As it happens, Wimsatt and Beardsley might with equal point have quoted him to epitomize their argument that an author's intentions are irrelevant. This, for example:

> Playes in themselues haue neither hopes, nor feares,
> Their fate is only in their hearers ears . . .[11]

It chimes in perfectly with the very end of Congreve's prologue although, here, his irony is too heavy to miss:

> In short, our Play shall (with your leave to show it),
> Give you one instance of a Passive Poet.
> Who to your Judgments yields all Resignation;
> So Save or Damn, after your own Discretion.

To link Congreve with Jonson is to place his prologue and what it says in a developing tradition of the author's presence in his printed works. In that context, Congreve's lines become a form of homage to his mentor, an acceptance of succession, and a reminder that the fight for the author's right not to be mis-read can ultimately break even the best of us. For not only had Jonson inveighed against the usurpation of *his* meanings by those of his asinine critics, but he was a dramatist who for a time virtually quit the public stage to be, as he put it, 'Safe from the wolues black iaw, and the dull asses hoofe'. Jonson's rejection of free interpretation is venomous:

> Let their fastidious, vaine
> Commission of the braine
> Run on, rage, sweat, censure and condemn:
> They were not meant for thee, lesse, thou for them.[12]

Congreve's ironies allow him a more tactful, more decorous, farewell. Less tough, more delicate, than Jonson, he did leave the stage, sensing himself expelled by the misappropriation of his works, convinced that *his* meanings would rarely survive their reception. The imminence of that decision informs his prologue to *The Way of the World*. It was to be his last play. On '*mature Deliberation*', he found he could no longer bear the deadly '*Dulness*' of his critics. By respecting not only the words Congreve uses – a simple courtesy – but also the meanings which their precise notation gives, we can, if we wish, as an act of bibliographical scholarship, recover his irony, and read his pain.

In that long series of Pyrrhic victories which records the triumphs of critics and the deaths of authors, 'The Intentional Fallacy' has earned a distinguished place for the argument which follows its feat of misprision. Its epigraph is no celebration of Congreve's perspicacity in foreseeing a new cause; it is, rather, an epitaph to his own dismembered text. A vast critical literature has been generated by this essay, but I am unaware of any mention of the textual ironies which preface it. With what seems an undue reverence for the tainted text printed by Wimsatt and Beardsley, the epigraph has been reproduced in reprint after reprint with exceptional fidelity, its errors resistant to any further reworking of a classic moment of mis-statement, resistant even to the force of the argument which follows it. It is now incorporate with Congreve's history and with that of our own time.

Yet if the fine detail of typography and layout, the material signs which constitute a text, do signify in the ways I have tried to suggest, it must follow that any history of the book – subject as books are to typographic and material change – must be a history of misreadings. This is not so strange as it might sound. Every society rewrites its past, every reader rewrites its texts, and, if they have any continuing life at all, at some point every printer redesigns them. The changes in the way Congreve's text was printed as an epigraph were themselves designed to correct a late Victorian printing style which had come to seem too fussily expressive. In 1946, 'good printing' had a clean, clear, impersonal surface. It left the text to speak for itself.

This newly preferred form of printing had conspired with shifts in critical opinion. Eliot's theory of the impersonality of the poet affected to dissociate the writer from his text. The words on the page became what Wimsatt called a 'verbal icon', a free-standing artefact with its own inner coherence, what Cleanth

Brooks was to call (as it happens) a '*well-wrought Urn*', a structure complete in itself which had within it all the linguistic signs we needed for the contemplation of its meaning.

The unprecedented rise of English studies and the decline of classics made quite new demands of teachers of literature. At one level, the critical analysis of set texts was an efficient way to teach reading from what was irreducibly common to a class, the text itself laid out on the page in a kind of lapidary state. At another level, it brought into sharper focus than ever before the fact that different readers brought the text to life in different ways. If a poem *is* only what its individual readers make it in their activity of constructing meaning from it, then a good poem will be one which most compels its own destruction in the service of its readers' new construction. When the specification of meaning is one with its discovery in the critical practice of writing, the generative force of texts is most active. In that context, the misreading of Congreve in 1946 may be seen as almost a matter of historical necessity, an interesting document itself in the nature of reading and the history of the book.

And it *is* a physical document. We can date it; we can read it; we can locate it in the context of *The Sewanee Review* and the interests of its readers; we can interpret it reasonably according to the propositional intentions of the anti–intentionalist essay which lies beneath it. It is, I hope, unnecessary to multiply instances. This scrap of prologue, this fragment of text, raises most of the issues we need to address as we think about books as texts which have been given a particular physical form.

But as a dramatic text, it was originally written to be spoken, and so other questions arise. Can we hear the voice of Thomas Betterton conveying orally the ironies we now read visually? Congreve's autograph letters show no concern for the niceties I suggested in the form of the epigraph. Am I therefore reading an interpretation of Congreve's meaning by his printer, John Watts? Is Watts merely following a general set of conventions imposed at this time, with or without Congreve's assent, by Congreve's publisher, Jacob Tonson? Who, in short, 'authored' Congreve? Whose concept of the reader do these forms of the text imply: the author's, the actor's, the printer's, or the publisher's? And what of the reader? Is a knowledge of Jonson, Betterton, Congreve, Watts, and Tonson a necessary condition of a 'true' reading? Does my reading betray a personal need to prove that a technical interest in books *and* in the teaching of texts, is not radically disjunctive, that bibliographical scholarship and criticism are in fact one? Visited by such questions, an author disperses into his collaborators, those who produced his texts and their meanings.

If we turn to the 1946 epigraph, similar questions insist on an answer. Does its removal from context entirely free it from irony? Do the slight changes of form alter the substance? Are they no more than a case of careless printing in a new convention? But the crucial questions for a history of reading, and the re-writing of texts, are these: did the intentions of these two authors (something extrinsic to their text) lead them to create from Congreve's lines a pre-text for their own writing; and, if so, did they do it consciously, unconsciously, or accidentally?

To venture into distinctions between conscious and unconscious intentions would be to enter upon troubled waters indeed. The probable answer is, I fear, banal, but as an illustration of the vagaries of textual transmission it should be given. The anthology of plays edited by Nettleton and Case, from which Wimsatt would almost certainly have taught, includes *The Way of the World,* the prologue to which in that edition inexplicably reads 'wrote' for '*wrought*'. We must therefore, I think, relieve Wimsatt and Beardsley of immediate responsibility, and we should certainly free them from any suggestion of deliberate contamination. But I wonder if they would have ventured to choose the lines had they been more carefully edited.[13]

The case, however, is not altered. If we think of the physical construction of Congreve's text in the quarto of 1700 or the octavo edition of 1710, and its physical re-presentation in 1946, then at least we begin by seeing two simple facts. One gives us the historical perspective of an author directing one set of meanings in a transaction with his contemporaries. The other gives us an equally historical perspective of two readers creating a reverse set of meanings for an academic – indeed, a scholarly – readership whose interests in the text were different. Each perspective can be studied distinctively in the signs of the text as printed. Those signs range in significance from the trivial to the serious, but far from importing the author's irrelevance, they take us back to human motive and intention. In Congreve's case, they reveal a man of compassion whose scenes record the human struggle they spring from as the very condition of writing.

In one sense at least, little has changed in critical theory since 1946. New Critical formalism and structuralism on the one hand, post-structuralism and deconstruction on the other, all share the same scepticism about recovering the past. One of the most impressive objections to this critical self-absorption, to the point of excluding a concern for the complexities of human agency in the production of texts, is Edward Said's *The World, the Text, and the Critic*. I can only agree with his judgement that 'As it is practised in the American academy today, literary theory has for the most part isolated textuality from the circumstances, the events, the physical senses that made it possible and render it intelligible as the result of human work'.[14] Commenting upon Said in his most recent book, *Textual Power*, Robert Scholes pursues the point: 'At the present time there are two major positions that can be taken with respect to this problem, and . . . it is extremely difficult to combine them or find any middle ground between them'.[15] Scholes describes those two positions as the hermetic and the secular.

To return now to my larger theme: Greg's definition of what bibliography is would have it entirely hermetic. By admitting history, we make it secular. The two positions are not entirely opposed, for books themselves are the middle ground. It is one bibliographers have long since explored, mapped, and tilled. Their descriptive methods far surpass other applications of semiotics as a science of signs. In the ubiquity and variety of its evidence, bibliography as a sociology of texts has an unrivalled power to resurrect authors in their own time, and their readers at any time. It enables what Michel Foucault called 'an insurrection of subjugated knowledges'.[16] One of its greatest strengths is the access it gives to social motives: by dealing with the facts of transmission and the material evidence of reception, it can make discoveries as distinct from inventing meanings. In focussing on the primary object, the text as a recorded form, it defines our common point of departure for any historical or critical enterprise. By abandoning the notion of degressive bibliography and recording *all* subsequent versions, bibliography, simply by its own comprehensive logic, its indiscriminate inclusiveness, testifies to the fact that new readers of course make new texts, and that their new meanings are a function of their new forms. The claim then is no longer for their truth as one might seek to define that by an authorial intention, but for their testimony, as defined by their historical use. There was a year 1710 in which Tonson published Congreve's *Works,* and there was a year 1946 in which some lines from the prologue to *The Way of the World* were quoted in *The Sewanee Review.* Wimsatt and Beardsley might be wrong from Congreve's point of view, but, given their published text, they indubitably *are*, and it is a very simple bibliographical function to record and to show their reading – indeed, in the interests of a history of cultural change, to show it up.

Reviewing Scholes in *The Times Literary Supplement,* Tzvetan Todorov gave a blunt appraisal of the relation of the present American literary scene to the traditions of western humanism: 'If we wish to call a spade a spade, we must conclude that the dominant tendency of American criticism is anti-humanism'.[17] Bibliography has a massive authority with which to correct that tendency. It can, in short, show the human presence in any recorded text.[18]

'Droeschout's First Folio Shakespeare' by Nicholas Wade. Reproduced from *Word and Image.* 1985, I, no.3, p.259. ▶

To the Reader.

This Figure, that thou here seest put,
  It was for gentle Shakespeare cut;
Wherein the Grauer had a strife
  With Nature to out-do the life:
O, could he but haue drawne his wit
  As well in brasse, as he hath hit
His face; the Print would then surpasse
  All, that was euer writ in brasse.
But, since he cannot, Reader, looke
  Not on his Picture, but his Booke.

                    B.I.

T   Reader.

This Figu   here seeſt put,
  It was   Shakeſpeare cut;
Wherein the Grauer had a ſtrife
  with Nature,   doo the life :
O, could he but he drawne his wi
  As well in braſſe, as he hath his
His face, the Print would then ſurpaſſe
  All   was euer writ in braſe.
But, ſince he cannot, Reader, looke
  Not on his Picture, but his Booke.

                    B. I.

II

The broken phial: non-book texts

THE ALLUSION in the phrase 'The broken phial' is of course to the famous passage in Milton's *Areopagitica,* where he speaks of books as having 'a potencie of life', for 'they preserve as in a violl the purest efficacie and extraction of that living intellect which bred them . . . a good book is the pretious life-blood of a master-spirit, imbalm'd and treasur'd up on purpose to a life beyond life'.

Milton's use of the word 'violl' is interesting, since, in the Greek, it usually meant a broad, flat vessel, like a saucer; and in the Authorized Version it is still translated as a 'bowl'. The sense of its being a small glass bottle, containing an essence, seems to have developed in the Seventeenth Century. I have not pursued the inquiry further but I imagine that this meaning relates to the use of glass tubes and phials in scientific experiments. Their transparency would have been important for allowing one to read the level of a liquid, as we do in a thermometer or mercy-glass, or to see chemical reactions involving, for example, changes of colour.

In this rather new sense, then, as used by Milton and later by Boyle, it heightens the idea of enclosure, of the text as contained, determined, stable, of the author within, both clearly visible and enduringly present. When we note Milton's spelling of the word, we see that it may also bear another meaning which we lose if we modernize it. Given the spelling of the 1644 edition ('violl'), and Milton's delight in music, there cannot be much doubt that we have here a typical Miltonic pun: it is as if, in reading a book, we should also be moved by the harmony of the work, what Shakespeare called 'the concord of sweet sounds'.

In such phrases, Milton puts most clearly the idea of the book as a sacred but expressive form, one whose medium gives transparent access to the essential meaning. As I tried to suggest earlier, there is a tradition in which print-inclined authors assume this. They use, or expect their printers to use, the resources of book forms to mediate their meaning with the utmost clarity. Even when writers, scribes, illuminators or illustrators, printers and publishers, merely accept the conventions of their time, with no innovative or specific intent, there are still certain codes at work from which, if we are sensitized to them, we can recover significant meanings we should otherwise miss or misinterpret.

Against that tradition, however, which is ultimately Platonic, if not Hebraic, for at one level it accepts the reality of a pure inner voice, and at another, a realm of absolute truth, of ideal forms, there is of course a counter-tradition which is also Hebraic and Platonic. If God said, 'Let there be light' and there was light, writing has interposed a dark glass which obscures the light which was the voice of God. The precious life-blood of Milton's master-spirit is inevitably watered down as it is spread around. As Shakespeare puts it in 'Phoenix and the Turtle':

> Truth may seeme, but cannot be;
> Beautie bragge, but tis not she . . .

In a mutable world, absolutes, by definition, are rare birds. We know them only by report, and all reported information must suffer what the telecommunications engineers call 'transmission-loss'.

Plato himself made this point most delightfully in *The Symposium*. Socrates there remarks that 'it would be very nice, Agathon, if wisdom were like water, and flowed by contact out of a person who had more into one who had less'. But such, of course, is not the way of things. The event Plato records as a symposium is filtered down to us ten years later through Apollodorus, who was not even there. Apollodorus, whose memory in any case, we are told, is rather hazy, is merely trying to recall what he was told by an equally vague Aristodemus, whose recollection of what Socrates had said Diotima had said, was scarcely reliable. To unsettle us further, we are told that the text of *The Symposium* as we have it is only a selection of bits from one particular version. As Apollodorus says, it relates only 'the most important points in each of the speeches that seemed to me worth remembering'. Any hopes that we might have had of the alternative version are instantly dashed, for it was, in its turn, only a garbled account that Glaucon says he had from Phoenix who was not there either but who, like Apollodorus, had heard it from Aristodemus. To do him justice, Apollodorus checked out the odd detail with Socrates, but in the light of a recital like that, the claim by Barthes that the birth of the reader demands the 'death of the author', is again, like all European intellectual history, only another foot-note to Plato.[1]

Within that counter-tradition, not only is any recorded text bound to be deformed by the processes of its transmission, but even the form it does have is shown to be less an embodiment of past meaning than a pretext for present meaning. Plato is often cited as one who deplored the shift from speech to script, and in *The Phaedrus* he is of course quite explicit about this. But he does in fact have it both ways. *The Symposium* is not only a brilliant piece of writing, but, as a memorializing act, its forms resurrect and make more of a night with Socrates than Alcibiades ever enjoyed.

To come closer to our own times, the relegation of writing to the indeterminate and endlessly transforming processes of textual dissemination is a by-product of Saussurian linguistics and some of the structuralist theories built upon it. In privileging the structures of speech over those of script, it displaced the older, text-based, philological, diachronic study of language, in favour of purely synchronic analysis – how people talk now. This shift in attention away from the study of historical process makes it easy to conclude that we cannot really presume to recover an authorial voice at all, or an intended meaning, from the written or printed records of it. We are left only with synchronic structures, and the conventions which regulate their meaning as we read. It follows, of course, that if the meaning we read is entirely a function of the structural relations within the verbal sign-system which constitutes a text, then it is not something in-herent which can be ex-pressed at all. Meaning is not what is meant, but what we now agree to infer.

Saussure's insistence upon the primacy of speech has created a further problem for book-based bibliography by confining critical attention to verbal structures as an alphabetic transcription of what are conceived only as words to be spoken. Other formalized languages, or, more properly perhaps, dialects of written language – graphic, algebraic, hieroglyphic and, most significantly for our purposes, typographic – have suffered an exclusion from critical debate about the interpretation of texts because they are not speech-related. They are instrumental of course to writing and printing, but given the close interdependence of linguistics, structuralism and hermeneutics, and the intellectual dominance of those disciplines in recent years, it is not surprising perhaps that the history of non-verbal sign systems, including even punctuation, is still in its infancy, or that the history of typographic conventions as mediators of meaning has yet to be written.

To revert briefly to Congreve, throughout that discussion one question was implicitly begged: could it be said that Congreve personally intended the meaning I read from his lines, or were the meanings I attributed to them more promiscuously generated? The question is both sceptical and anxious in its hope for reassurance. To keep alive that tension between disbelief and confirmation, I have kept in reserve Congreve's explicit assurance in the edition of 1710 that 'Care [had] been taken both to Revise the Press, and to Review and Correct many Passages in the Writing'. By way of general explanation, Congreve added:

> It will hardly be deny'd, that it is both a Respect due to the Publick, and a Right which every Man owes to himself, to endeavour that what he has written may appear with as few Faults, as he is capable of avoiding.

Not to be too philosophical about it here, such a statement gives us confidence to assume that, in his case, most of the forms we have in that edition were intended. To that extent, the meanings were implied and controlled. But it does not of course remove the problem. Any specific instance could be an exception. And readers themselves of course bring such different styles of readings to texts that they can quite easily elude the subtlest forms of direction. These different styles are, in some measure, culturally determined; and if a current theory of meaning holds that an author's voice is muted, the ideas *de*formed, by print, there will be a general disposition within the culture to act as if the detail of past intentions and the forms of their expression are relatively insignificant compared with present meanings.

By such arguments, the integrity of the author's text, its transparency, and the formal unity of the book which embodies it, implied in Milton's image of the phial, have been consistently broken down. Today, one reads rather of the *less* than sacred text, the destabilized, the indeterminate, or the open text.

Laurence Sterne made the point about the indeterminacy of texts in a beautifully urbane and comforting way in *Tristram Shandy*, but he made it none the less:

> . . . no author, who knows the just boundaries of decorum and good-breeding, would presume to think all: The truest respect which you can pay to the Reader's understanding, is to halve this matter amicably, and leave him something to imagine, in his turn, as well as yourself. For my own part, I am eternally paying him compliments of this kind and do all in my power to keep his imagination as busy as my own.

Peter de Voogd has recently drawn attention again to the marbled pages in the third volume of *Tristram Shandy*, which Sterne calls 'the motley emblem of my work'.[2] Each hand-marbled page is necessarily different and yet integral with the text. As an assortment of coloured shapes which are completely non-representational, a marbled page as distinct from a lettered one might even be said to have no meaning at all. Most modern editions, if they do attempt to include them, and do not settle merely for a note of their original presence, will print a black-and-white image of them which is uniform in every copy of the edition. By doing that, of course, they subvert Sterne's intention to embody an emblem of non-specific intention, of difference, of undetermined meaning, of the very instability of text from copy to copy. Marbled end-papers were common enough in fine bindings before Sterne's time, but by making his marbled page a textual feature, Sterne was clearly using a most forceful and innovative example of expressive form. In one sense, Sterne's principles and practice here confirm the idea of textual indeterminacy, but in fact, in the very moment of denying the authority of the author, the extraordinary specificity of a hand-marbled page deviously confirms it. Like Plato, Sterne has it both ways.

Bibliography, in Greg's definition, would of course have side-stepped all these problems of the indeterminacy of texts: its business, as we have seen, was simply to record and compare manuscript and/or printed versions. Textual criticism, however, could not quite so easily avoid it. Since it was thought that it must have as its object a 'true' text, one different from each of its defective versions, some notion of 'the text in a form its author intended' was indispensable.

In tune with the times, however, that concept too has largely collapsed. In textual criticism, the most obvious case of the unstable or open text is created by revision. Where an author revised a text, and two or more versions of it happen to survive, each of these can be said to have its own distinct structure, making it a different text. It embodies a quite different intention. It follows therefore that, since any single version will have its own historical identity, not only for its author but for the particular market of readers who bought and read it, we cannot invoke the idea of one unified intention which the editor must serve. Historically, there can be no logical reason for editing one version any more than another. We can make aesthetic choices, but that is a different matter. We can choose, if we wish, to privilege an author's second or third thoughts over his first, but we need not. The old idea that we should respect an author's final intentions no longer compels universal assent. The only remaining rule seems to be that we must not conflate any one version with any other, since that would destroy the historicity of each.

All this makes perfectly good sense in terms of *histoire du livre*. The versions are not only discrete but are telling evidence of a precise set of significances at successive points in history. But there is a curiously cautious, conservative dullness about it. On the one hand, it rejects the old idea of recovering 'the work' as distinct from its versions; on the other, it stops short in theory – though never in practice – of embracing the notion of creative editing in the construction of new versions. Such a policy may seem to be justified when we think that texts might be edited 'creatively' for political purposes.[3] But that argument is merely a disguised form of censorship and was sufficiently answered by Milton.

I find it more worrying that such a view of the function of textual criticism fails to account for 'intention' as a 'speculative instrument' (in I. A. Richards's phrase), a means of creating a master-text, a kind of ideal-copy text, transcending all the versions and true to the essential intention of the 'work'. In this sense, the work may be the form traditionally imputed to an archetype; it may be a form seen as immanent in each of the versions but not fully realized in any one of them; or it may be conceived of as always potential, like that of a play, where the text is open and generates new meanings according to new needs in a perpetual deferral of closure. Again, in terms of *histoire du livre,* this too makes perfectly good sense. History simply confirms, as a bibliographical fact, that quite new versions of a work which is not altogether dead, *will* be created, whether they are generated by its author, by its successive editors, by generations of readers, or by new writers.[4]

Faced with those possibilities, ranging from an author's manipulation of the most minute details of meaning in printed texts to the appropriation of texts as completely open to new constructions, the textual critic is in a sad case of compromise. A convenient statement of the kind of solution currently offered is that by Mr James McLaverty in a recent issue of *The Library:*

> The editor needs to respect the integrity of the different
> versions of a work, and he should consider himself free of duty
> of the author's final intention. On the other hand, he must try to
> establish the author's text, not that of the compositor or
> house-corrector.[5]

This does not entirely dispose of the concept of intention, but we
can see that it breaks it down by multiplying it out into distinct
synchronic structures and leaves us free to choose whichever one
we wish. In rejecting conflation, it disposes of a diachronic use of
intention as a structure of meaning which embraces two or more
successive versions. And, finally, it continues to cast doubt on the
printer's role.

These are not esoteric matters. Should you be inclined in future
to read Shakespeare's *King Lear* in the new Oxford edition, you
will have a kind of twistaplot choice between two versions, each
substantially different from the other, and both quite different
from the conflated text which we have hitherto read. If you wish
to be a do-it-yourself editor and construct your own text, the new
edition will provide you with a kit-set consisting of a couple of
virtual facsimiles of the versions which it declined to conflate (but
implies that you may). Like Plato and Sterne, we can have it both
ways.

At a moment like this, it is tempting to call in Aristotle's
distinction between history and poetry as a model of the problem.
History tells us what was: it records the versions. Poetry – the
more serious and philosophical art – tells us what *ought* to be. To
my mind, there is a moral imperative in that 'ought' which I
personally find compelling. It can function in two ways. It may
drive us, as historical scholars, to recover a 'true' text from the
detritus of versions; or it may direct us, as creative reader/writers,
to generate the meanings that most matter to us. In either case,
there is an act of creation involved. Even scholars read, and edit,
with a mission. Editors make, as well as mend. The text is, in
Terence Cave's word, cornucopian.

What price then Milton's phial? Even in those unspectacular

ways, we can see that critical experiment and textual theory have, at the very least, crazed and clouded the glass, if not shattered it. The moment we think of non-book texts, however, it breaks down altogether as an adequate symbol of the traditional book as the object of bibliographical and textual inquiry. What is clear is that Milton's concept of the book and of an author's presence within it represents only one end of a bibliographical spectrum. The counter-tradition of textual transformations, of new forms in new editions for new markets, represents the other. A sociology of texts would comprehend both. It would also extend their application to the scholarship of non-book texts.

To establish the continuity of bibliographical principle in non-book forms, however, is not easy, and of course it is quite impossible to do so even plausibly in the space of half a lecture. So again, one can only be pragmatic and indicative, pointing out what seem to be parallel cases, ones where the records have a textual function which is subject to bibliographical control, interpretation, and historical analysis. It may well be that, for present purposes at least, it is more convenient to think simply in terms of homologies, of correspondent structures, suggesting that, whatever our own special field – be it books, maps, prints, oral traditions, theatre, films, television, or computer-stored data bases – we note certain common concerns.

To put the case at its most extreme, we should certainly have to account for visual but non-verbal texts, as well as oral ones, both in our own culture and in non- or pre-literate cultures, as well as in what are now called a-literate communities, where there is a level of functional literacy, but where the written or printed text does not have the status still enjoyed by speech.

Let me begin then by asking if there is any sense in which the land – not even a representation of it on a map, but the land itself – might be a text. In their study of the Australian aboriginal tribe, the Arunta, Spencer and Gillen devote a chapter to totemic topography: every prominent feature of the landscape in the Arunta country is associated in tradition with some totemic group. 'Special rocks, caves, trees and creeks, that have a local totemic significance, are dotted over the whole country.'[6] It is not simply a matter of their being sacred objects, although they may be that too, but of their having a *textual* function. These visual, physical features form the ingredients of what is in fact a verbal text, for each one is embedded in story, has a specific narrative function, and supports in detail the characterization, descriptive content, physical action, and the symbolic import of a narration. Reverse the telescope, of course, and it is just like the allegorical reading of landscape in, say, *The Faerie Queene*.

At the western end of the Mount Gillen range in Arunta land is a small block of stone called *Gnoilya tmerga*. It stands

> in the middle of a wide-open flat, associated with a great, white, dog man who came from Latrika, away to the west, and wanted to kill all the dog men at Choritja. When they saw him, the local Gnoilya men sang out *Wunna mbainda erinna, numma* – see, this is your camp, sit down. So he sat down quietly and remained there, the stone arising to mark the spot. If the stone is rubbed by the old men, all the camp dogs begin to growl and grow fierce. The last man to rub it was one of the old Inkatas, who did so after the white men had come, in order to try to make the dogs bite them.[7]

A Eurocentric point of view does not make it easy to accept that landscape has a textual function, but, in that account, there is no way of dissociating its physical features from the narrative. The stone in its exact position means a story about the coming of the white men, and it implies a future in which the texts of the Arunta, the legends of their dreamtime, will be emended, not by scholars re-telling the story, but (as Dr Harold Love put it to me) by mining companies blowing up mountains in the search for minerals.

This is not, I think, too melodramatic a way of making a point about the nature of texts. Where the case for Aboriginal land rights is being most successfully made, against the literally entrenched opposition of those with mining rights, it is by virtue of the stories which the land holds, the codification in landscape of a whole tribal culture. It is the narrative power of the land, its textual status, which now supports a political structure dedicated to the belated preservation of the texts which make up a culture.

If we can but think the question through that way round, think not of books as the only form of textual artefact, but of texts of many different kinds in many different material forms, only some of which are books or documents, then we begin to see a principle at work which has quite staggering social, economic, and political implications. The argument that a rock in Arunta country is a text subject to bibliographical exposition is absurd only if one thinks of arranging such rocks on a shelf and giving them classmarks. It is the importation into Arunta land of a single-minded obsession with book-forms, in the highly relative context of the last few hundred years of European history, which is the real absurdity.

I am reminded of a story told about a member of Jesus College, Cambridge, which by virtue of its succession of very long-lived masters, had a prodigious collective memory. A recently elected young science fellow, so the story goes, was anxious to get a small reform through the Governing Body. But having been warned that, in the context of an Oxbridge college, nothing is trivial, from the placing of a comma to the misplacing of a napkin, he did his homework with great care. The time for the meeting arrived. When his item on the agenda came up, he took some pride in assuring those present that, just in case his proposal might be thought a little too radical, he had uncovered an interesting precedent in the college archives. In fact, so keen had he been to reassure them on this point, he had searched through all the records for the last 300 years and found nothing seriously inconsistent with his proposal. At which point, the Master lifted his head wearily and observed: 'But you would agree, would you not, that the last 300 years have been somewhat exceptional?'

For the Maori in New Zealand, the arrival of books and documents has made the last 150 years more than somewhat exceptional. Despite the fact that Keri Hulme has recently won the Booker Prize, texts in the form of written or printed documents are still widely distrusted. This is mainly because of the strength of oral traditions, but there is another, more sinister, reason. For many Maoris, the archetypal document – the Treaty of Waitangi of 1840, by which British sovereignty was secured over New Zealand – stands as a symbol of betrayal. It deprived them of their lands, and in taking their lands it threatened their culture. This is not a question of arguing a case, or proving a truth; it is a matter of daily living, or at least living daily with the consciousness of it. For the Maori, their relation to the land – epitomized in their phrase for those who belong to the land, *te tangata whenua* – continues to be the most important subject of debate, and land is significant, not for its commercial value – although that may now be a consideration – but for its symbolic status. A site is picketed, and public works on it opposed, more often to preserve its significance in myth and legend than out of material interest.

When looking into the implications of introducing printing into New Zealand, the attempts to make the Maori literate, and European exploitation of the legal power of documents over agreements reached orally, I had occasion to look at the Maori 'signatures' appended in 1840 to the Treaty of Waitangi. Some are signatures in the usual sense of the word, but most are complicated configurations.[8] A suggestion worth exploring further is the possibility that these forms of writing may in fact be representations of natural features of the tribal lands from which the signatories came. For the British at the time, their textual significance was crucial, because in European terms these little maps – if such they are – signified assent to their assumption of sovereignty. But if, for the Maori, they signified tribal lands over which they thought they would continue to have sovereign control, under the queen's protection, then these enigmatic signatures may yet prove to be territorial texts of some potency.

In such signs we can see the idea of place hovering between the verbal and non-verbal but rising, as it were, to textual significance. The sign of the land here makes a man.

The same kind of indeterminate relation between indexical sign and symbolic meaning applies to maps. If, instead of trying to decide what makes them different from books, we were instead to seek out the similarities of maps with other forms of text, we could note to begin with that the specification of place-names is clearly a linguistic feature. As such, these elements in maps are subject to the normal processes of record and comparison, to establish a line of transmission or an affinity of versions. The adoption of a reformed spelling, the substitution of indigenous names for those of colonizing powers, the graphic location and scaling of names, their typographic relation to an implied use, are dimensions of symbolic meaning in the verbal text of a map. They may not make sentences, but they are messages. The principles of textual criticism apply no less here because the words are graphically, not grammatically or syntactically, defined. Difference, the essential ground of meaning in language, is here at least partly a matter of distance.

But what constitutes a text is not the presence of linguistic elements but the act of construction. As Roland Barthes says of texts as the materials of myth, all that is required is that they 'presuppose a signifying consciousness'.[9] Traditionally, a map has rarely shown what anyone can see: its relation to reality is like that of words to the world – almost entirely arbitrary, not mimetic. Just as we see a landscape because we have already named its parts and look for what we know – for 'valley, rock, and hill' – so maps take on meaning by virtue of the conventional understanding given to signs and their structure in a particular text. The most primitive expression of spatial relationships in a map is more symbolic than representational, since it must involve scale and the omission of detail. Celestial maps are testimony to a phenomenal power of compression. The flat map expresses an ingenuity most sharply expressed perhaps in the skills of projection. Illumination, colouring, shading, calligraphy, compass-points, lines of latitude and longitude, all testify to an increasing sophistication in the use of graphic devices as expressive forms. Another, in one sense arbitrary, convention in maps is their selectivity, the decision to select certain features, but not others, by which to represent a milieu. Different maps tell very different stories, and assume very different forms, according to their function, or their point of view. Ptolemy mapped the heavens by standing on earth. Galileo remapped them by imagining that he was standing on the Sun. They are not, therefore, subject-specific, any more than books, photographs and films are. Nor are they material-specific. Nor do they deal uniquely in spatial relationships, since many kinds of graphic and kinetic images do that.

We are all indebted to the work of Sarah Tyacke for tracing, in

35

the history of British maps, an important overlap with the book trades.[10] For the making, distribution and sale of maps has, like that of musical scores, been only a specialized instance of a larger trade in the production of texts, whether as manuscripts, block–prints, copper–plates, etchings, lithographs, or photographic images, on paper or any other material of widely different qualities, using type, ink, printing presses, book formats, subscription publishing, and so on, exploiting a range of markets, both domestic and foreign. The use of maps with a narrational or explicatory text, as in accounts of voyages, whether real or imaginary, is only another instance of how each mode of word and image shares something of the other's nature in story-telling.

To mention the map trade is to imply a market and therefore an intended use. Maps also raise all the questions of intention and reader-response, without at the same time engaging the complexities which arise from the exceptional ambiguity of that special class of texts which we call literary. With maps, the deliberation with which devices are used to define meaning is clear. They establish precise relationships between the physical phenomena represented within the map as text, and, by assuming a 'correct' reading, they also establish a precise relationship between the reader and the text. And yet they can also pluralize reading. For example, once define a feature by colour and the long–established principle of colour-separation makes it perfectly easy to print out a version of a map which gives only, say, rivers, or only railway lines, and so on. In other words, colour is both a combinative creative tool in permitting multiple readings of the same text, as well as multiple relationships within it (for example, the crossing of a blue river and a black railway line implies – or at least it had better imply – the new reading 'bridge'), but it also permits a series of, as it were, deconstructed readings of individual features.

Not ten years ago, in their book on the nature of maps, Robinson and Petchenik could still resist the idea that the information system within a map was either a language or a text: 'The two systems, map and language', they wrote, 'are essentially incompatible'.[11] Their objections were the familiar ones that language is verbal ('meaningful patterns of vocal sounds' is their definition), that images do not have a vocabulary, that there is no grammar, and that the temporal sequence of a syntax is lacking. That definition of language logically entails a limited concept of text:

> As is true of the reader of text, the map percipient understands some of the intended information on the basis of a complex interaction of eye and brain. But certain differences between the text reader and the map percipient are fundamental: the text reader must follow a particular sequence in his acts of visual perception, and he must relate his visual stimuli to a system of sounds and meanings rather than to another system of visual images. If one merely 'looks' at an array of letter-figures, the process is never called 'reading'. The map percipient, in contrast, can and does enter the graphic array at any point; he can stop at any point; and often he relates the visual stimuli to other visual stimuli, rather than to a system of sounds.[12]

For them, maps are silent, visual, spatial, and a-temporal. I am not myself concerned to argue that maps are a language in that narrower sense, merely that as constructions employing a conventional sign system they constitute texts, and that, not as books but as texts, bibliographical principle embraces them too. More recent writers will have taken account of developments in the theory of language systems, but it is unfortunate that the two principal theorists of mapping resisted the more inclusive uses of the concepts of language and text. They had already been employed by, for example, film theorists who had to work through many of the same problems of definition and general theory. I think in particular of Christian Metz, whose 1968 *Essai sur la signification au cinéma,* available in English since 1974 as *Language and Cinema,* has dealt with them in detail.[13]

I must make it clear that I speak of maps only as someone stimulated to inquire into certain parallels with a field I am more familiar with. It does seem, for example, that the arrival of the orthophotomap, which presents an image of the 'natural' surface, raised much the same kind of question about the object 'map' as computer-stored information now raises about the object 'book'. So too does what I believe is called 'remote sensing and digital mapping'. Computerized cartography must involve highly intentional programming and the manipulation of graphics in ways which also create a temporal sequence, as indeed did celestial maps in the form of the astrolabe or concentric globes, with the help of which astrologers have been reading the heavens for centuries. The creation of map images by electrical impulses, as for example from outer space – but it could be along any land-line – involves the use of sound in a physical medium translated into light. It is not quite voice into graphics, but the definitions of even ten years ago begin to look decidedly feeble. The metaphorical use of the word 'map', as in 'mapping out a project', is easily extended to concepts other than a milieu, and as easily reproduced in screen graphics as is a traditional map.

Should we not at least be asking questions about the bibliographical control of weather maps, which shift their forms ceaselessly on the living-room screens of 98% of the population, or at which point one stops a kinetic image to keep a record for posterity? But these problems are common to all forms of text, certainly of all performative ones, and it is at that level of abstraction, I believe, that we should collectively be thinking how to deal with them. Future historians of cartography, concerned to produce for climatologists a record of the transitions from one state of the climate to another, may find them deficient, their stemmatics frustrated, by our failure to devise an adequate bibliographical principle to deal with them.

But to return to ways in which maps may signify as texts, it is I think worth remarking the obvious for its human implications: that the signs, whether verbal or non-verbal, may also express ideological meanings. As such they can function as potent tools for political control or express political aspirations. The visual adjacency of territories, the border-line definition of linguistic, ethnographic, religious, or political boundaries, may be an accurate record of the current facts, but the four forms seldom correspond exactly. A visual definition in terms of any one may be a subversive political act in terms of another.

Brian Friel's play *Translations* is a perceptive study of these dimensions of maps as texts and of the economic, political and cultural implications of naming. Its action takes place in 1833 at a hedge-school in an Irish-speaking community in County

Donegal, where a recently arrived detachment of the Royal Engineers is making the first Ordnance Survey. For purposes of cartography, 'every hill, stream, rock, even every patch of ground which possessed its own distinctive Irish name' had to be Anglicized, 'either by changing it into its approximate English sound or by translating it into English words. For example, a Gaelic name like Cnoc Ban could become Knockban or – directly – Fair Hill'.[14] It is a play full of implications for my own country where, only this year, the Maori officially reclaimed one of New Zealand's most beautiful mountains from British cartography which had made it Egmont. As Taranaki, it now resumes its older history.

The question is one of the status of images as texts. It has now been so fully explored by William Ivins and Roland Barthes that perhaps there is not really any further resistance to it. Ivins's analysis of the significance of technological processes in determining how we read an image – how, for example, the engraving of paintings destroyed their texture and stressed instead their composition and iconography – was a remarkably prescient account of things to come.[15] Barthes has simply taken the analysis further by establishing the continuity of photography with prints. The camera may have rendered redundant the interpretive skills and conventional sign systems of draughtsman and engraver, but in at least two ways the photograph functions textually as an interpretive construct.

First, any photograph is now recognized as yet another artifice: the frame selects the content; further selections of film stock, lens, filter, aperture, exposure and light, set physical limits to the form of the image; any number of modifications can be introduced during development, which may affect all or only part of the image; and, of course, paper quality, size of print and the milieu in which it is seen, will also determine the readings it gets.

Second, as Barthes demonstrates to great effect, the photograph only signifies at all 'because of the existence of a store of ready-made elements of signification (eyes raised heavenwards, hands clasped)'. These continuities have of course a long history, not only in the graphic expression of emotion but in the rhetoric of gesture. When he reads Garbo's face, or the Roman fringe in

Mankiewicz's film of *Julius Caesar,* he finds a cultural text. In 'Photography and Electoral Appeal', he writes: 'the full-face photograph underlines the realistic look of the candidate, especially if he is provided with scrutinizing glasses'; and 'almost all three-quarter face photos are ascensional, the face is lifted towards a supernatural light which draws it up, and elevates it to the realm of a higher humanity . . .'.[16]

Such comments now seem almost naive when we think of the manner in which we are exposed to the professional encoding of 'sincerity' in advertizing and politics, but Barthes did a service in bringing past practice into line with new technology and exposing the true nature of the texts we were reading.

The same time-honoured devices of manipulative display can be found more overtly in comic-strip Shakespeare. Words become noisy with visual sound (ARRGH!!, in caps, double exclamation mark), and the sectional division of the action into frames – as in the Strasburg *Terence* of 1493 – almost puts the pictures into motion. 'There are sudden cuts of time and place, rapidly shifting camera angles, a mix of long shots and close-ups, a whole range of montage effects.'[17] But, unlike the motion picture, you can stop the action, flip it back and forth, change the emphasis and tempo, take up a full page for an expansive, liberating image, cram it with small panels to create a sense of claustrophobia, sharpen the angles to express paranoia, or use splitting-images to suggest the schizophrenic. The positioning of balloons to give the temporal sequence of lines is ingeniously contrived to create a text which, like theatre itself, combines the verbal, visual, gestural and colourful, in yet another regeneration in response to what publishers conceive as new – as one might say – cultural needs.

I hasten to add that I am not endorsing the form as a suitable one for Shakespeare, but simply stressing the point that such a construction of words and graphics is a complex, composite text, which seeks to impart in print at least some of the elements of performance.

The relation of textual criticism to the realities of theatrical production has always been one of embarrassed impotence. The dramatic text is not only notoriously unstable, but, whatever the script, it is again never more than a pre-text for the theatrical occasion, and only a constituent part of it.

The sources of such an event are the dramatist, director, designer, composer, technicians; its messages are conveyed by body, voice, costume, props, set, lights; the signals are made in the form of movements, sound, colour, even smells; light waves and sound waves channel the messages of speech, gesture, music, and scenic forms to the senses – mainly the eyes and ears – of an audience. These reader–receivers will interpret them variously and respond with laughter, tears, yawns, applause, whistles, boos, or even by leaving early. Those responses in turn sustain, or disturb, the actors in their roles. As Thomas More pointed out, if audience and actors fail to observe the conventions which allow this complex text to come into being, there is utter confusion. The range of codes and subcodes at work here is extremely wide. They function in movement, space, costume, make-up, setting, music, architecture, rhetoric, as well as in the ideolectal ways in which individual actors work, and in the dialectical relationships of the play's themes, or of the company which performs it, to the community for which it is written.

In many ways, it is those last considerations – if you like, the sociological dimension of production and reception – which confirm the textual nature of each element in a play. Under certain conditions of censorship, for example, colour can be highly significant; and of course a theatrical event includes almost all the features of oral performance skills, from repetition to extemporization and audience inter-play. It is in a context like this that texts are perhaps best seen, not as fixed, determined artefacts in a specific medium, but as potential. All the versions imply an ideal form which is never fully realized but only partly perceived and expressed by any one. As such, the dramatic text, like Sterne's concept of *Tristram Shandy,* differs only in degree from the dynamic forms of computer graphics.

When speaking of Panizzi in a recent BBC programme on the British Library, Mr Alex Wilson said:

> I think if Panizzi were alive today – as I say to some of my more traditionally-minded colleagues – *he* would be more radical,

more adventurous, more outward looking, have the biggest
computer of the lot. He was a man for change and adaptation, as
well as a man for tradition.[18]

That seems to me absolutely right. And Panizzi, who, we should
now recall, edited Ariosto's *Orlando Furioso* and Bojardo's
Orlando Innamorato, would not, I think, have simply accepted
computing as just another technological aid, one more efficient
than others for doing certain jobs. He would have asked: on what
unifying, intellectual principle, does it relate to books? The
Reading Room itself has become, of course, the figure of the man
in expressing his perception of the unity of knowledge. But I
should like to remind you of its much earlier expression in his
study of Ariosto:

> The general opinion has been, that the *Orlando Furioso* is a
> collection of several poems on distinct subjects; and the number
> as well as the denomination of these subjects, is determined
> according to the idea which each critic or commentator has
> formed of the work. But no one has hitherto tried to discover
> whether there might not be in the *Orlando Furioso* one main
> subject on which all the others depended, or from which they
> were derived; whether the different branches of this stately tree,
> although so widely spread, might not be all proceeding from a
> single stem, concealed from the eye by their own luxuriant
> foliage.[19]

If I might apply the figure in an aptly Renaissance manner: that
principle of unity Panizzi was seeking in the *Orlando Furioso* is no
less the subject now of bibliographical inquiry. What seem to be
the different branches, each with its own luxuriant foliage, are the
several media in which texts are stored and transmitted. But the
single, hidden stem, the source of the animating principle which
flows in each different branch, is the text.

To apply the figure even more specifically, I should like to take
a recent example which reflects on the relationship between
computers and books, and may affect any one of us.

As of 11 November 1985, under the *Data Protection Act, 1984,*
some 400,000 computer users in Britain were required to register

in compliance with the law to protect individuals from the misuse of personal data stored on computer. As from March 1986, anyone may seek compensation through the courts for damage and distress caused by the loss, destruction, inaccuracy, or unauthorized disclosure of information, and they may emend the text by having inaccurate records corrected. As from November 1987, they will have right of access to personal information stored about them on computer. But those rights of legal redress, correction and access do not apply to the identical information – the same text – if it is stored in the traditional, written, type-written, multi-layered, paper file.

One can, of course, understand the arguments from expediency for such a distinction – considerations of ownership, scale, ease of access, and so on. But of any two individuals differently affected by the different manner in which information about them is stored, one might well feel that some central, unifying concept of 'the text' had broken down. One individual will have access, and legal redress, and can revise the text; the other will have none, and cannot. In arguing for the centrality of a textual principle in bibliography, whatever specific form the text takes, I am not denying that we must ultimately return to the fine detail of each kind of text and the professionalism, the scholarship, proper to it; but just at this time it seems more needful than ever to recover the unity in their otherwise disabling diversity.

In that same rich text of his which deals with so many of these questions, Milton reassures those made anxious by the division of Truth into parties and partitions. 'Fool!', he exclaimed to one of them, see you not 'the firm root out of which we all grow, though into branches?'

III

The dialectics of bibliography now

IN THE first two lectures I briefly contrasted two concepts of 'text'. One is the text as authorially sanctioned, contained, and historically definable. The other is the text as always incomplete, and therefore open, unstable, subject to a perpetual re-making by its readers, performers, or audience.

To stress the first is to confirm the usual assumptions of historical scholarship: it seeks, as objectively as possible, to recover, from the physical evidence of a text, its significance for all those who first made it. To do that, I have argued, we must have some concept of authorial meaning, consider carefully the expressive functions of the text's modes of transmission, and account for its reception by an audience or readership. As a locatable, describable, attributable, datable and explicable object, the text as a recorded form is, pre-eminently, a *bibliographical* fact. Its relation to all other versions, and their relation, in turn, to all other recorded texts, are, again, pre-eminently, bibliographical facts. No other discipline – and certainly neither history nor criticism – commands the range of textual phenomena, or the technical scholarship, to deal fully with their production, distribution and consumption. By commanding the one term common to all inquiry – the textual object itself – bibliography can be an essential means by which we recover the past.

As a way of further exemplifying one part of that argument – the relation of form to meaning in printed books – I should like to consider the cases of John Locke and James Joyce. Locke was so troubled by the difficulty he had in making sense of St Paul's epistles, that he decided to go right to the heart of the matter. In 1707 he published *An Essay for the Understanding of St. Paul's Epistles. By Consulting St. Paul himself.* In this essay he quite explicitly addresses the question of intention, and the role of typographic form in obscuring or revealing it. More than that, he implies that if we do not get these things right, they can have the most serious social and political effects. He ascribes his problems in reading the epistles to:

> *The dividing of them into Chapters and Verses, . . . whereby they are so chop'd and minc'd, and as they are now Printed, stand so broken and divided, that not only the Common People take the Verses usually for distinct Aphorisms, but even Men of more advanc'd Knowledge in reading them, lose very much of the strength and force of the Coherence, and the Light that depends on it.*

Locke objects to the eye being '*constantly disturb'd with loose Sentences, that by their standing and separation, appear as so many distinct Fragments*'. As he develops it, his argument about editorial and typographic practice, has far-reaching implications:

> *. . . if a Bible was printed as it should be, and as the several Parts of it were writ, in continued Discourses where the Argument is continued, I doubt not that the several Parties would complain of it, as an Innovation, and a dangerous Change in the publishing of those holy Books. . . . as the matter now stands, he that has a mind to it, may at a cheap rate be a notable Champion for the Truth, that is, for the Doctrine of the Sect that Chance or Interest has cast him into. He need but be furnished with Verses of Sacred Scriptures, containing Words and Expressions that are but flexible . . . and his System that has appropriated them to the Orthodoxie of his Church, makes them immediately strong and irrefragable Arguments for his Opinion. This is the Benefit of loose Sentences, and Scripture crumbled into Verses, which quickly turn into independent Aphorisms.*

Those comments make it clear that Locke believed the form in which a text was printed not only radically affected the ways it might be read, but might even indeed generate religious and civil dissension. He then raises the whole question of authorial intention. As printed in verse, the epistles frustrated those sober, inquisitive readers who had a mind like his own *'to see in St. Paul's Epistles just what he meant; whereas those others of a quicker and gayer Sight could see in them what they please'*. For Locke, an essential condition of following a true meaning was a proper disposition of the text, so that one might see *'where the Sense of the Author goes visibly in its own Train'*. He then adds:

> *And perhaps if it were well examin'd, it would be no extravagant Paradox to say, that there are fewer who bring their Opinions to the Sacred Scripture to be tried by that infallible Rule, than bring the Sacred Scripture to their Opinions, to bend it to them, to make it as they can, a Cover and a Guard for them. And to this Purpose its being divided into Verses, and being brought as much as may be into loose and general Aphorisms, makes it most useful and serviceable.*

One finds these points repeatedly confirmed in all popular debates on moral issues. The most recent in my own experience is that about a Homosexual Law Reform Bill before the New Zealand Parliament, where, for nearly a year, members shot biblical verses from one side of the House to the other like paper darts in a school-room. Their substance was equally puerile, they made a mess, demeaned serious debate, and generated passions which led to serious civil disturbance. It was an exact replay in 1985 of Locke's argument of 1707.

Some less contentious illustrations of this relation between book forms and textual meaning may be drawn from the work of James Joyce. The 1984 'critical and synoptic' Garland edition of *Ulysses* has been welcomed as an impressive work of scholarship.[1] It offers in effect a parallel reading of the novel, to which it imputes a 'many-layered and highly complex text that carries the dynamics of an extended textual development within it'. On one page we have an editorial de-construction of the documents into their successive moments of transmission and modification by typists, printers, and by Joyce himself as he corrected proof. This is imaged on the facing page by a new construction of the work, one presumed to be implicit in the bewildering, genetic detail which opposes it, but with an explicit claim to an authority higher than that of any completed form known to Joyce. This, it is claimed, is 'the emended continuous manuscript text at its ultimate level of compositional development'.

Given the evidence which it chooses to present, what the new edition could not do was to represent the physical form of *Ulysses* as it was first published. I have therefore been intrigued to learn recently from Dr John Kidd of ways in which the 1922 edition shows Joyce working to make textual meaning from book forms, rewriting in proof in a creative interplay with the fall of the text on the page, and nudging it into patterns of page-to-text, which offer markers, boundaries and divisions directly related to its final 'book' form. Being largely peculiar to that edition, these corres-pondent readings are automatically lost in any new setting which does not keep the identical form. They are therefore lost from the new edition, simply because its physical form is incompatible with them.[2]

Some suspicion that Joyce, of all authors, would put the medium of the book to work might have been aroused by the consciousness he shows in *Pomes Penyeach*. His superstition about the number 13 is well attested ('This year is to be incessant trouble to me', he wrote in 1921 to Harriet Beacher Weaver, adding in parentheses '1 + 9 + 2 + 1 = 13'). His mother died on 13 August 1903, and when he came to publish the poem which he wrote about her death in *Pomes Penyeach,* he placed it 13th in the book and called it 'Tilly' – as in the phrase 'Twelve and a Tilly', or a baker's dozen. Its 12 lines of text and one of title repeat the idea of both acknowledging and denying the reality of the number 13 and its associations. The price of *Pomes Penyeach* was a shilling, or 12 pennies for 12 poems, with the 13th free.

For that example and those that follow, and for permission to use them here, I am indebted to Dr Kidd. The first few are small, indicative ones. On reading a letter from his daughter Milly, who had just turned 15 on 15 June, Bloom says 'Fifteen yesterday. Curious, fifteenth of the month too'. More to the point, Joyce's revision in proof gives the letter 15 sentences. But every editorial attempt to 'correct' Milly's adolescent syntax and punctuation, by reverting to earlier versions, has of course changed the count and obscured the point. So too, the passage in which Bloom reflects on the rate at which an object falls to earth ('thirty-two feet per second') is heavily revised in print to make it the 32nd sentence in the paragraph, where reversion to earlier readings, as in the 1984 edition, obscures that convergence of sign and sense. On p.88, Joyce added in proof a sentence of eight words to expand a newspaper death notice. It reads: 'Aged 88, after a long and tedious illness'. To p.77 he added in proof the phrase 'seventh heaven'; and on p.360, Bloom meditates on cycles.

It is a commonplace that *Ulysses* retails the experience of one day and one night in a lifetime, as well as of a whole lifetime compressed into that single day and single night. But those general correspondences emerge more finely in the way Joyce develops them in proof. 1904 was a leap year. Since it is mentioned four times in the book, Joyce must have been highly conscious of it. The total number of days and nights in a leap year happens to be twice 366, or 732. The text of the 1922 edition of *Ulysses* falls on precisely 366 leaves or 732 pages. In a personal letter to me, Dr Kidd writes:

> [It] also divides evenly into diurnal and nocturnal halves. The sun sets in the seaside 'Nausicaa' chapter, not with a sudden plunge, but with a gradual waning, until daylight and Leopold Bloom's consciousness are extinguished on page 365. The remainder of the book is set in darkness. . . . Bloom, seated where shore and sea meet, attending the last glimmer of midsummer light, and remarking the semicircular profile of Dublin Bay, thinks there must be a divine order at work: 'Done half by design.'

That symmetry last appeared in the Odyssey Press edition of *Ulysses,* published in Hamburg in 1932. It was issued in two volumes. The final section of the first volume includes the phrase 'Done half by design.' signalling the reader to move on to volume two, the night volume, after a full day with Bloom.

Dr Kidd's examples do, I think, illustrate the force of at least one half of my argument: that books *can* be expressive forms of some subtlety, and that an editorial policy which ignores that fact is likely to bring forth a text which, by its author's standards, is deficient. I have no wish to criticize the recent Garland edition, which has its own distinct purpose. But I am pleased to learn of Dr Kidd's intention to publish a corrected facsimile of the 1922 Shakespeare and Company edition. Joyce engineered its publication date to fall on his birthday. He received the first two copies that day, the second of the second, 1922. Some Joyce scholars may be ruefully reflecting that on this day of the year one also celebrates the feast of the purification.

I should like now to move back to that other, contrasting, concept of 'text' and its nature as open, unstable, indeterminate. In this sense – a sense in which the recent editors of *Ulysses* have employed it – the 'text' is in some degree independent of the documents which, at any particular moment, give it form. It is to recognize too that no text of any complexity yields a definitive meaning. The ostensible unity of any one 'contained' text – be it in the shape of a manuscript, book, map, film, or computer-stored file – is an illusion. As a language, its forms and meaning derive from other texts; and as we listen to, look at or read it, at the very same time we re-write it. The word 'text-book', as first defined by Bailey in 1730, reminds us of this truth: '*Text-book* (in Universities) is a Classick Author written very wide by the Students, to give Room for an Interpretation dictated by the Master, &c. to be inserted in the Interlines.' Each student makes his or her own text.

That recognition brings us full circle. Whatever its meta-morphoses, the different physical forms of any text, and the intentions they serve, are relative to a specific time, place and person. This creates a problem only if we want meaning to be absolute and immutable. In fact, change and adaptation are a condition of survival, just as the creative application of texts is a condition of their being read at all. The 1984 critical and synoptic text of *Ulysses* has physically changed every previous version in the act of replicating it. It has become in its turn a new *bibliographical* fact; and it is these facts which constitute the primary evidence for any history of meanings. They alone make possible, in their sequence, any account of cultural change. Perceived from a bibliographical point of view, therefore, the ostensible contradiction between those two concepts of 'text', the closed and the open, simply dissolves. But implicit in those comments are several points about the nature of bibliography which it might be helpful now to make quite explicit.

First, I imply that it is committed to the description of all recorded texts. In principle, it is comprehensive, and therefore indiscriminate. Any national collection formed largely by copyright deposit shows this non-elitist, non-canonical, non-generic, all-inclusive principle at work. International networking simply extends it. Ultimately, any discrete bibliography of subject, person or collection merely contributes to an ideal of that universal bibliographical control. It thereby enables the discovery of any possible relationship there might be between any one text and any other text – whenever, wherever, and in whatever form. In other words, bibliography is the means by which we establish the uniqueness of any single text as well as the means by which we are able to uncover all its inter-textual dimensions.

Second, because it is bibliography's job to record and explain the physical forms which mediate meaning, it has an interpretive function which complements and modifies any purely verbal analysis. In principle, it can fulfil this function in any of the modes in which texts are transmitted, not just printed books. It is therefore equally relevant, as a discipline, to any structure of meaning which is recordable and discernible.

Third, it impartially accepts the construction of new texts and their forms. The conflation of versions, or the writing of new books out of old ones, is the most obvious case. But the construction of systems, such as archives, libraries, and databanks, is another. In every case, the elements from which they are constructed are bibliographical objects. A test case would be the sale and dispersal of, say, the library of a Seventeenth-Century scholar: we become acutely aware at such moments of a library's status as a text or a meta-text, and of its biographical and intellectual meaning.

Fourth, bibliography is of its nature, and not merely as a partial effect of some more essential function, concerned specifically with texts as social products. The human and institutional dynamics of their production and consumption, here and now, as well as in the past, have therefore led me to suggest that we might find in the phrase 'a sociology of texts' a useful description of its actual scope.

I must now turn to some exemplary cases of non-book texts and at least try to set out my reasons for thinking that bibliography has a duty to these. In doing so, it is worth recalling, I think, Hobbes's comment in *The Leviathan* that

> The Invention of *Printing,* though ingenious, compared with the invention of *Letters,* is no great matter. . . . But the most noble and profitable invention of all other, was that of SPEECH, consisting of *Names* or *Appellations,* and their Connexion.[3]

He reminds us here of what we are now having to re-learn: that print is only a phase in the history of textual transmission, and that we may be at risk of over-stating its importance. The relatively recent introduction of printing into non-literate societies has seldom endorsed our traditional view of its efficacy as an agent of change. Even in our own society, oral text and visual image have not only enjoyed a continuity (albeit, enhanced by print), but they have now resumed their status as among the principal modes of discourse with an even greater power of projection. The origins of that revival are much older than we might care to recall: the telegraph and photograph, telephone and phonograph, and even the motion picture itself, are all Nineteenth-Century inventions. In retrospect, the failure to develop forms of bibliographic control, adequate archiving, and proper public access on the model of the traditional library is understandable. But the cumulative force of those new media, together with even more recent ones like television, magnetic tape, optical disc, and computers, and the significance of the texts recorded in them, are now such that further neglect is inexcusable.

A social historian, writing 20 years hence about the need for, and the political appeal of, say, 'law and order' policies in the 1980s, would find the traditional texts of novels, plays, newspaper reports of football violence, official records of the parliamentary debates and legislation, relevant and accessible. But they would be quite incomplete without some account of television. I think in particular of a clip from a recent news item. A class of small children were being asked if they liked to watch programmes which had lots of violent action in them. One small boy's eyes lit up as he told the reporter how exciting he found it, how it made him feel that he wanted to be strong like that, to run in and kick, and knock people down. 'What do you want to be when you grow up?' asked the reporter. The instant reply was: 'A policeman'. I am not concerned here to pursue the interpretation of that text, but I am concerned to note that it *is* a text, and that future access to it might prove extremely instructive, not only about our present society, but about the nature of the one we may have become 20 years hence. But I cannot be sure how easy it might be to see a full range of films, or relevant television programmes; and the chances of a particular newsclip surviving in an easily accessible form are even more problematic.

In many ways, the film and video tape are the most complete summation of a tradition of oral, visual, and written and typographic communication. As the forms of text most immediately accessible to non-literate or a-literate societies, they perhaps make the most urgent demands of traditional bibliography for its descriptive methods, and its skill in conserving and accessing textual records. Films are deliberated, composed works in their total organization; as completed texts, they are objects more amenable to complete study than, say, unrecorded speech or a theatrical event. They have a physical length, a temporal span, and repeatable presence. Their use of sound, image, colour and movement makes them an ideal starting point for the extension of bibliographical principle from book to text.

But I think it is only proper to select an undisputed classic in which to explore the analogies I should like to draw, and indeed, in the year of his death, to turn in tribute to the work of Orson Welles, in particular of course, to *Citizen Kane*. It is a film I think which might be familiar to most of us; certainly it is one of the few to be given high canonical status, and therefore to have an unusually rich supporting literature.

It opens and closes with a literal sign, an image that is both verbal and visual. It is posted outside Kane's immense mansion of Xanadu, and reads 'NO TRESPASSING'. It is a playful image of enclosure, a detail of the film's tight textual construction, and of the intimate reciprocity of its verbal and visual text. Xanadu is no true pleasure dome. Reviewing the film in 1946, Borges saw in it the familiar structure of the centreless labyrinth, a world of fragments without unity, a recurrent symbol of the archive, the library, the museum, posing the same challenge to order, creating the same fears of failure.[4] With the prodigality of a Huntington or a Folger, or in this case even more pertinently a Pierpont Morgan, Kane poured into Xanadu specimens of the world's treasures in the hope of modelling in them a system which eluded him in life.

Lying old and ill in their still *dis*-ordered midst, Kane dies muttering the word 'Rosebud'. We hear it in his 'old, old voice' at the start of the film, which then proceeds by flashback to recover the story of his life, the business of what Pauline Kael has called 'raising Kane'.

In hopes of pinning down the meaning of the enigmatic 'Rosebud', a reporter resurrects Kane's public life by running a nine-minute newsreel made up of clips of its main events, but this ostensibly factual source of evidence, the contemporary record of 'News on the March', turns out to be as fragmentary and as full of false emphases as the printed newspapers which Kane himself published. As if to prove yet again that the truest poetry is the most feigning, Welles's own film supplants the newsreel as the source of truth. In doing so, it re-presents the 'news' in its true complexity with a clarity and a penetration which shows up the coarse conventions at work in the documentary record.

Welles can re-present and date those conventions all the more readily because flashback in films has always required a high consciousness of sign systems in order to establish a difference from the narrative present. It is a resource that Woody Allen exploits to hilarious effect in *Zelig* and *The Purple Rose of Cairo*. The first, if you are so inclined, may be read as a parody of all historical scholarship; the second, of all post-structuralist criticism. But my point of course is that films use, in a way more accessible than in books, formal systems of datable signs to recover the past. The conventions change with extreme rapidity, as we can tell from our own experience of re-viewing an old film we had thought quite natural when first we saw it. What once seemed to have the innocence of truth betrays – before long – an embarrassing artifice.

The press reporter's search for the explanation of 'Rosebud' is frustrated. Oral witness fails too in its variant versions of the same events. The documentary 'facts' are silent. Only as the film ends, and we see a workman toss an old sledge into a fire, do we catch a glimpse of the answer in the period lettering of the word 'Rosebud' painted on the sledge. It is a trite, sentimental, novelettish note, but in it Kane's voice becomes visible. The verbal image takes on graphic form, and like the script itself becomes the necessary complement to the non-verbal, visual constructions, which would fail of meaning without it.

As a text, *Citizen Kane* generates a critical dialogue which has numerous affinities with literary criticism. In its counterpointing of an elusive past with a questing present, its contrasting of the sub-literary genres of newsreels and newsprint with the high-culture of the canonical art-film, in its posturing with hermeneutics as the search for meaning within a closed structure, it is as fruitful a subject for critical inquiry as most printed texts. If that seems too solemn an account of its range of interests, then we can find in its cinematic poetry, as we can in *The Dunciad,* a vulgar, rumbustious, and always entertaining satire on the muck-raking press as one aspect of the social history of printing and publishing. Indeed, in its own attack on William Randolph Hearst, it imitates its subject. Those themes are not trivial, and they are recorded in a form which is so central now to the experience of our society, in particular that of the students who will be tomorrow's scholars, as to warrant an advanced scholarship to serve it.

Such a scholarship might note in Orson Welles himself the role, familiar in publishing, of the outsider as a significant source of innovation, the problems of funding, the threats of libel actions, the plot to buy up the film before its release and destroy the negative and all the prints; the formal features of the finished film, the semiotics of its textual detail; the constraints of censorship – indeed, the film's effectual suppression during the McCarthy era; the versions of the script, and subsequent re-releases; the manner of its distribution, the history of its reception; the annotational realm of Kane as a figure of Hearst, of the character Thatcher as J. P. Morgan junior, as well as the allusive plundering of the film by a generation of other directors.

The film is a total social fact and a total text. Film-makers, spectators and critics all think in terms of films as texts, because only some such word makes sense of the discrete parts of which a film is constructed. The concept of a text creates a context for meaning. In other words, we are back to the initial definition of text as a construction, and discover that, however we might wish to confine the word to books and manuscripts, those working in films find it indispensable. There is, I think, no profit to be gained by disputing the point: one accepts that the word now has a meaning which comprehends them all. Those who wish to contain it by confining it to books are like Milton's 'gallant man who thought to pound up the crows by shutting his Parkgate'.

Film theory of the 1960s and 1970s was still strongly influenced by structuralism in one way which bears significantly on my own argument about 'pure' bibliography (in the Greg-Bowers sense) and historical bibliography or the sociology of texts. In discussing photography, for example, Roland Barthes drew a distinction between the finished artefact as a closed construction and its context:

> The emission and reception of [a photographic] message both lie within the field of sociology: it is a matter of studying human groups, of defining motives and attitudes, and of trying to link the behaviour of these groups to the social totality of which they are part.[5]

The message itself, he claimed, had a structural autonomy in what it signified, and describing it was the business of semiotics. So too Christian Metz drew a distinction between the film as a textual system (whether confined to a single film or extended to the infinite text of what we call genre) and the cinema, which is the whole social complex of a film's production and consumption. It is my contention of course that this distinction ultimately fails, since the definition of meaning – in reading the conventional details of a text – is logically dependent upon prior decisions and social effect. Like typography as a conscious, interpretive skill, every presentational feature of a film is calculated to express symbolic meaning. It is unceasingly deliberate in its selection, shaping and pointing of significance.

Since it bears on the parallel I am suggesting between books and films as expressive forms, I should like to take up this last point with a comment from Gregg Toland, the director of photography for *Citizen Kane*. In 'How I broke the Rules in *Citizen Kane*', he makes a distinction between 'photographic commands and conventions in shooting the picture':

> Photographically speaking, I understand a commandment to be a rule, axiom, or principle, an incontrovertible fact of photographic procedure which is unchangeable for physical and chemical reasons. On the other hand, a convention, to me, is a usage which has become familiar through repetition. It is a tradition rather than a rule. With time, the convention becomes a commandment, through force of habit. I feel that the limiting effect is both obvious and unfortunate. With those definitions in mind, I'll admit that I defied a good many conventions in filming *Citizen Kane*.[6]

That is precisely what Congreve and Tonson must be said to have done in designing Congreve's *Works* (1710). The analogy here with the technologies of print in relation to the finished book could be pushed further by a more technical discussion of how Welles altered our perception of reality by obtaining an unusual depth of field, of the experiments with high-speed film stock, the treating of the lens surface to eliminate refraction, the use of the twin-arc broadside lamp, the lap dissolves and their relation to the foregrounding or backgrounding of images, or the composition of shots. All those technical details are of course peculiar to the construction of film texts, not books, but their function is still to create meanings by the skilled use of material forms. In that, and in the relation of technology to expression, I think the parallel holds. But it may be more readily granted in the area of description.

Pauline Kael has edited the final shooting script of *Citizen Kane* dated 16 July 1940, and the subsequent so-called cutting continuity. She explains the difference between them as that of before and after:

> The shooting script is written before the film is shot – it is the basis for the film; the cutting continuity is a stenographic record made from the finished film. Cutting continuities tend to be impersonal and rather boring to read, and if one examines only the cutting continuity it is difficult to perceive the writers' contribution. Shooting scripts are much more readable, since they usually indicate the moods and intentions.[7]

Her use of the word 'intentions' is only the most immediate note of a congruence with the traditional concerns of bibliography and textual criticism. The relationship of the shooting script to the finished script is much like that of a manuscript draft, not even perhaps a fair copy, to a printed text, whereas the more boring cutting continuity comes closer to the iconic record of a bibliographical description.

There are three versions of the shooting script as preserved in the Museum of Modern Art in New York. Another, described as the second, revised final script, date 9 July 1940, and earlier than any of the other three, was submitted to the Production Code Office for clearance. It passed the test except for some four or five details. One of them recalls the effects on Shakespeare's text of the Act of Abuses of 1606: 'Please eliminate the word "Lord" from Kane's speech ". . . the Lord only knows . . .".' Another puts one in mind of Polonius, concerned lest his son 'enter such a house of sale, *Videlicet,* a brothel', because there was such a place nominated as a locale for set C. But the Production Code demanded that it be dropped. What it is important to know, as an aspect of Welles's intention, is that the scene had only been written in for trading purposes in the sure knowledge that it would have to be cut, but in the hope that other, less obtrusive, items would then slip through, as they did.

Pauline Kael reprints the shooting script as revised, although there is no table of variants. What we do have are brief notes on departures from the script as the film was made. Then there is the RKO cutting continuity, dated 21 February 1941. Its apparatus consists of a brief note ('Slightly amended to correct errors in original transcription'), but for the rest, it represents a version of the full film text which, in default of being the film itself, is a bibliographer's dream of iconic accuracy. Like a description of ideal copy, it enables one to test all actual copies in the minutest details for sequence and completeness. For example, to correspond with the authentic version, a copy must run for one hour, 59 minutes, 16 seconds. But I have seen one release for television cut to less than that. There are seven reels, each divided into numbered scenes. The left-hand entries in the description are details of the length of each of these in feet; in the centre are notes on the scene, the camera's and the actors' movements, and, under centred speech headings, the dialogue; on the right, is a description of the manner in which the scene is changed.

To anyone familiar with the making or teaching of films, these details are commonplace. Again, my concern is merely to establish the point that the older disciplinary structures of bibliography, in the description of books and the construction of texts from the extant versions, are closely comparable to those required for film, and that the common interest is at this stage served by acknowledging that the discipline comprehends them both. It is ironic that in an age when type for books is film-set, and when, for purposes of storing the information content of books, we would now turn them into photographic images on plastic, the film itself should still be labouring for bibliographical and textual attention. Those which get it, like *Citizen Kane,* are the rare exception.

Bibliographers – as 'pure' bibliographers – may of course continue to insist on making a rigorous distinction between books as we commonly know them and non-book forms, and on the restriction of 'pure' bibliography to description and analysis of the book as a physical object. But libraries – and especially national libraries, with a responsibility to the culture at large, past, present, and future – are under significant pressure to evolve systems which accommodate these new forms of text in a rational, coherent, stable and yet socially accessible way.

The pattern is already pragmatically there in the transformation of our personal and city libraries. Some of us still buy books, of course; but we also borrow them, and we have left to the public conscience and public institutions the responsibility for preserving the newspapers and periodicals that we dispose of. Most of us have music, and could have videos, on disc or tapes, and the machines required to hear and see them. We are beginning to store information at home in our own computer files, or to buy access to other systems. That principle of buying access is simply an extension of the old idea of the lending library: we do not buy the book so much as the time in which to read it. With new forms of text, we buy, in bulk, the reading, viewing, or listening time in the form of an entrance fee to the cinema, a hiring fee for the disc or video, or a wireless and television licence fee for all or any texts that might be made and transmitted in the year ahead, or we pay an access fee for the information in a data bank. By decision of the United States Supreme Court, it is no infringement of copyright there to record television programmes in order to shift time. But in fact the technical capacity most consumers now command – as readers, listeners, or viewers – to copy texts in that way, has also in part transformed the notion of purchase as a form of acquisition and the ways in which – some of us at least – form our personal libraries.

Such reflections form the terms of an all too familiar litany over the demise of the book. My concern is different. It is to find the continuity of these forms with past forms, of our new libraries with past libraries in their traditional function as collectors, conservators, classifiers and communicators, as classically exemplified by Panizzi. Even the use of computer technology to supply information changes in only one respect that traditional function. Whereas libraries have held books and documents as physical objects, computer systems have been mainly concerned to retrieve content. Library conservation and inter-lending policies are already pushing certain classes of existing document into that mode; and the creation and supply of new texts in non-printed form for direct consultation on screen, or subsequent hard-copy print-out, is increasing. The principle of record and access, of catalogue and holdings, is not changed but only refined. It is too seldom remarked that library systems influenced computing in the development of its capacity to process basic catalogue functions by symbolic listing, selection, and arrangement. It should also be remembered that it was not the sophistication of computing in its early stages which biased its use towards science, but its limited memory and therefore its inability to handle the complexity and range of verbal language as distinct from combinations of the numbers 0 to 9. Only as its memory systems have grown has the computer changed its nature from blackboard to book. It has at long last become literate and qualified to join other textual systems. In time, I suppose, as it now learns to speak, it will constitute an oral archive as well.

But one consequence of the computer's retarded development for many years has been a much slower recognition of the essential consonance of its functions, like that of other non-book texts, with the traditional purposes of libraries. Large, long-established, institutional structures are not notable for their ability to adapt rapidly to changed conditions, but if a common principle can be perceived and acted upon, it does at least open up to us a politically important leadership role. Once that is acknowledged, it is not a question of creating a monolithic institution with the curatorial role of preserving all forms of text (the National Sound Archive is part of the British Library; the British Film Archive is not). What is important is the promotion of inter-institutional collaboration in the pursuit of a common aim, and the proper provision at last for the archiving and accessing, the bibliographical control, of the new kinds of text.[8]

That reflection returns me to film as my chosen case. The concept of the archive has of course been recognized now in the use of the name in several countries. Where 'film library' implies active lending and limited retention, the 'film archive' implies the primacy of a custodial function and a principle of access restricted to conditional consultation. But despite much individual, dedicated work, it is rare to find resources available on a scale commensurate with the need. MARC standards have been set by the Library of Congress for the description of films, but books remain privileged over them, and in default of political imperatives with matching resources, the application of standards – as in my own country – is at best fitful or highly selective. Although films enjoy the benefits of copyright protection, in neither Britain nor New Zealand is there any provision for their legal deposit. What is done is again done by personal or commercial initiative, without legal sanction, and usually without adequate funding for archiving in the full range of its obligations. The problems of access can therefore be acute. They range from the philistinism which, in the name of commerce, has completely destroyed artefacts of outstanding merit, to mutilation by censorship, cutting, gross imping out with commercials, or the private retention or suppression of cultural documents of such quality and significance that they should be in the public domain.[9] In the 1960s, British television drama, in quality of scripting, performance and production, was of a standard it has rarely achieved since. But it might be difficult to prove the point because many of the programmes have been destroyed. After the exact number of transmissions for which, by contract, the performers had been paid, Equity rules required the master and all copies to be destroyed lest the contract be infringed by later, unauthorized transmissions.

I think those conditions force us to ask: 'What principle, if it is *not* a bibliographical principle, determines questions of authority, transmission, and reception in all those cases? And in what measure must a *public* library as the traditional custodian of books, and bibliography as the relevant discipline, take up the cause for such texts?'

I stress 'public' because commercial considerations rarely bear upon the past with much responsibility to historic depth. There are basically three points: copyright, storage, and access. Copyright deposit puts all specified works into the public domain and thereby ends all the uncertainties that informal and private arrangements are heir to. Storage will always be costly of space and labour, if the original artefacts are to be kept. Just as vellum manuscripts were scraped clean for re-use, so too are magnetic tapes vulnerable to re-use, with the destruction of the texts already in them. A principle of economy in the service of private interest renders all records vulnerable. Why keep them if the demand year by year diminishes to the point where they are seldom consulted and it becomes unprofitable to maintain the structures which house and service them? Even in the public realm, some texts are more equal than others, a principle of frequency of use is invoked, and policies of selective retention constantly advocated. But even given deposit and proper storage, access to original artefacts which are machine-specific will need batteries of historic equipment on which to re-play them. In fact, it is more likely to involve the frequent re-copying (and, by a well-known textual principle, their gradual degeneration?) to make them compatible with new technology.

Those considerations suggest that only a traditional, bibliographically informed concept of library service, dedicated to the public interest as a matter of principle and not of profit, will effect the preservation of such texts, guarantee their authenticity, and ensure access to them.

I hope it is unnecessary for me to stress my personal interest in bibliography as the study of books and their history, but I hope there is no mistaking either the earnestness with which I have been concerned to argue the case for a comparable attention to other forms of recorded texts. I may be mistaken in my premises and in my logic, but I have tried to argue the case in terms of principles and continuities as I have come to experience them. The book as we know it will, of course, remain an important form of text – for many purposes, the most important. I want nothing to do with fashionable claims that – as Tom Stoppard might have put it – the pages of the book are numbered. I am well aware that, when we are so committed to the force, indeed here to the encircling presence, of their tradition, it seems impossible, this side of tragedy, to live without them. And yet there has always been that counter-mythology which has affirmed the demands of the world, against those of the book.

We find it at work even in such a bookish novel as Umberto Eco's *The Name of the Rose*. You will remember that a bibliographical curiosity there flowers into life as Eco reconstructs from it an elaborate figure of the ingeniously ordered, but labyrinthine, Alexandrian archive, only to deconstruct it again in the old and fearful symbolism of the library as a furnace. Fire consumes the books. As it rages, the librarian as jealous conservator of knowledge, the reader (if you like) as bookworm, literally – letter by letter – eats the sole text of Aristotle's treatise on comedy in a desperate effort of enclosure. It is a last-ditch denial of the multiple life of the text as a communal property, the ultimate image of the library as a closed-book system. At the same time as it disappears from view into its only reader, the text itself, unique and therefore indistinguishable from the poisoned state of its physical form, consumes and destroys him as it becomes wholly his. The moral is deadly: we can become too absorbed by books.

Brilliant though it is, the factitious density of its inter-textual comedy has *The Name of the Rose,* like all accounts of texts and their readers, ending up as just another fiction about a non-existent text, yet another story (so to say) of Echo and Narcissus.

By contrast, Marlowe's *Faustus* gives us, perhaps, the most poignant statement we have of the tragedy which books can entail. When this scholar Faustus selects his texts and constructs from them his own version, his book of the self, he reads his way to hell.

> *Ieromes* Bible, *Faustus,* view it well.
> *Stipendium peccati mors est:* ha, *Stipendium, &c.*
> The reward of sinne is death: thats hard.
> *Si peccasse negamus, fallimur, & nulla est in nobis veritas.*
> If we say that we have no sinne,
> We deceiue our selues, and theres no truth in vs.
> Why then belike we must sinne,
> And so consequently die.

Faustus reads in Jerome only a single sense dictating a fixed fate. What he omits are the words that refer to mercy, the very foundation of which – if I may so put it – is the variant reading, an openness to interpretation, a deference to the spirit in preference to the letter. Trapped by the paradox that texts are both closed and open, fixed and flexible, defined by one context only to be redefined in others, Faustus despairs. Instead of using judgement, he suffers it; and with his agonized cry – 'I'll burn my books' – he rejects the whole tradition of book-learning.

Of all the traditional enemies of books in this counter-mythology, none are so powerful as fire and water. These will devour sense, or drown it, with more dextrous celerity than a whole cortège of critics. If Faustus invokes the one, it is Prospero who invokes the other.

The Tempest towers above all other texts as an exposition of the instrumentality of the book, a key to open the mysteries of nature, a tool to oppress and confine the savage mind. Prospero makes plain how much they meant to him when he recalls Gonzalo who,

> of his gentleness
> Knowing I lou'd my books, . . . furnish'd me
> From mine owne Library, with volumes, that
> I prize aboue my Dukedome.

And yet one of the most remarkable perceptions in that spare but infinitely generative play is Prospero's even greater need to surrender his power, and with it the books which bestowed it:

> And, deeper than did euer Plummet sound
> Ile drowne my booke.

Encased by his library, he had shut out the world.

> Me (poore man) my Librarie
> Was Dukedome large enough . . .

At the heart of the English Renaissance, a period unprecedented for its readerly-ness and writerly-ness, two voices warn us that books are not always enough.

It seems a simple point to end on, but the times again give it proof. As the British Library begins like Prospero to dismantle itself, and surrender its magic circle for the square, its redefinition as a library of texts, verbal, numeric and visual, and in many different media, is also imminent. Defining the ways our world might use them, the structure that orders them, and the future scholarship that they must serve, will demand of bibliographers more than I think we currently offer. It asks no less than a new concept of the text in history.

1 'Bibliography – an Apologia', in *Collected Papers*, ed. J. C. Maxwell (Oxford: Clarendon Press, 1966), p.247.

2 Ross Atkinson, 'An Application of Semiotics to the Definition of Bibliography', *Studies in Bibliography* 33 (1980), 54–73.

3 *Bibliography and Textual Criticism* (Oxford: Clarendon Press, 1964), p.41; cited by Atkinson, p.63.

4 'Bibliography and Science', *Studies in Bibliography* 27 (1974), 88.

5 Principally in 'Bibliography, Pure Bibliography, and Literary Studies', *Papers of the Bibliographical Society of America* 47 (1952), 186–208; also in 'Bibliography', *Encyclopaedia Britannica* (1970), III, 588–92.

6 Atkinson, p.64.

7 *Encyclopaedia Britannica*, III, 588.

8 Nicolas Barker, 'Typography and the Meaning of Words', *Buch und Buchhandel in Europa im achtzehten Jahrhundert*, ed G. Barber and B. Fabian, *Wolfenbütteler Schriften zur Geschichte des Buchwesens* 4 (Hamburg, 1981), pp.126–65; Giles Barber, 'Voltaire et la présentation typographique de *Candide*', *Transmissione dei Testi a Stampa nel Periodo Moderno* I (Seminario Internationale, Rome 1985), 151–69; Roger Laufer, 'L'Énonciation typographique au dix-huitième siècle', ibid., 113–23; 'L'Espace visuel du livre ancien', *Revue Française d'Histoire du Livre* 16 (1977), 569–81; 'L'Esprit de la lettre', *Le Débat* 22 (November 1982), 147–59; see also Barbara R. Woshinsky, 'La Bruyère's *Caractères*: A Typographical Reading', *TEXT, Transactions of the Society for Textual Scholarship* 2 (1985), 209–28. Those examples from the past, implying a consciousness of the non-verbal resources of book forms to enhance and convey meaning, may be paralleled with others from current research into text design. A useful recent summary is James Hartley, 'Current Research on Text Design', *Scholarly Publishing* 16 (1985), 355–68; see also James Hartley and Peter Burnhill, 'Explorations in Space: A Critique of the Typography of BPS Publications', *Bulletin of the British Psychological Society* 29 (1976), 97–107.

9 For an excellent example, see Michael Camille, 'The Book of Signs: Writing and visual difference in Gothic manuscript illumination', *Word & Image* I, no.2 (April–June 1985), 133–48.

10 *The Sewanee Review* liv (Summer, 1946), 468–88; subsequently collected in *The Verbal Icon* (Lexington: University of Kentucky Press, 1954).

11 Ben Jonson, *The New Inne*, epilogue, ll. 1–2.

12 'Ode *to himselfe*', ll. 7–10.

13 I am indebted to Professor Albert Braunmuller for suggesting the probable source of the error. In fairness to Wimsatt and Beardsley, whose matching essay, 'The Subjective Fallacy', warns against readings uncontrolled by the

formal limits of the words on the page, it should be said that they might well have welcomed and accepted as constituting a more acceptable text the lines as originally printed.

14 *The World, the Text, and the Critic* (London: Faber and Faber, 1984), p.4.

15 *Textual Power* (New Haven and London: Yale University Press, 1985), p.75.

16 Michel Foucault, 'Two Lectures: Lecture One: 7 January 1976', in *Power/Knowledge: Selected Interviews and Other Writings 1972–77*, ed. Colin Gordon (Brighton: Harvester Press, 1980), p.81.

17 'Against all humanity', *Times Literary Supplement*, 4 October 1985, p.1094.

18 The photo-construction is by Nicholas Wade. It appeared in *Word & Image* I, no.3 (July–September 1985), 259.

NOTES TO LECTURE II

1 Roland Barthes, 'The Death of the Author', in *Image, Music, Text: Essays Selected and Translated by Stephen Heath* (London: Fontana, 1984), p.148. Michel Foucault, in 'What is an Author?', raises many of the same questions as does Barthes, but his essay seems to me far more sympathetic to the range of concerns which have traditionally preoccupied those interested in the non-authorial dimensions of textually transmitted knowledge. It appeared originally as 'Qu'est-ce qu'un auteur?', followed by a discussion, in *Bulletin de la Société Française de la Philosophie* 63 (1969).

2 Peter de Voogd, 'Laurence Sterne, the marbled page and "the use of accidents" ', *Word & Image* I, no.3 (July–September 1985), 279–87.

3 For a development of this point as it might be applied to a specific political problem, see D. F. McKenzie, *Oral Culture, Literacy, and Print in Early New Zealand; The Treaty of Waitangi* (Wellington: Victoria University Press, 1985), pp.45–47.

4 Literature on the psychology of reading is indicative. See, for example, Marlene Doctorow, M. C. Wittock, and Carolyn Marks, 'Generative Processes in Reading Comprehension', *Journal of Educational Psychology* 70 (1978), 109–18.

5 *The Library*, 6th series, vi (June 1984), 138.

6 B. Spencer and F. J. Gillen, *The Arunta . . . a Stone-Age People*, 2 vols (London: Macmillan, 1927), I, 88. I am indebted to Dr Harold Love for this reference.

7 ibid. I, 92.

8 A sample may be seen in *Oral Culture, Literacy, and Print*, pp.38–39.

9 'Myth Today', in *Mythologies: Selected and Translated from the French by Annette Lavers* (London: Granada, 1984), p.109.

10 See, in particular, Sarah Tyacke, *London Map-Sellers 1660–1720: A collection of advertisements for maps placed in the 'London Gazette' 1668–1719 with biographical*

notes on the map-sellers (Tring: Map Collector Publications, 1978); Sarah Tyacke and John Huddy, *Christopher Saxton and Tudor Map-making* (London: The British Library, 1980); and *English Map-Making 1500–1650: Historical Essays,* ed. Sarah Tyacke (London: The British Library, 1983).

11 Arthur H. Robinson and Barbara Bartz Petchenik, *The Nature of Maps: Essays toward Understanding Maps and Mapping* (Chicago and London: University of Chicago Press, 1976), p.43.

12 ibid. p.45. On this point, see Camille, 'The Book of Signs', p.135: 'the best form of representation for refuting the arguments for the non-linguistic nature of visuality and for understanding how an image can function on the same complex semantic levels as a text is the medieval diagram. This was readable as *scriptura* and yet totally dependent on presentation through *pictura*'. See also J. B. Harley, 'Meaning and ambiguity in Tudor cartography', in *English Map-Making,* pp.22–45, especially note 103, p.45: 'a systematic study of 'carto-literacy' in early modern England is required along the lines of D. Cressy, *Literacy and the Social Order, Reading and Writing in Tudor and Stuart England* (Cambridge, 1980)'.

13 Christian Metz, *Language and Cinema* (The Hague: Mouton, 1974).

14 Brian Friel, *Translations* (London: Faber and Faber, 1981), p.34.

15 W. M. Ivins Jr, *Prints and Visual Communication* (London: Routledge and Kegan Paul, 1953).

16 In *Mythologies,* pp.92–93.

17 I quote from a review by Bill Manhire of editions of *Macbeth,* illustrated by Von, and of *Othello,* illustrated by Oscar Zarate (London: Sidgwick and Jackson, 1982, 1983), in *The New Zealand Listener,* 19 January 1985, p.34.

18 Broadcast on 18 November 1985.

19 Ariosto, *Orlando Furioso.* With memoirs and notes by Antonio Panizzi, 4 vols (London: Pickering, 1834), i, xcv.

NOTES TO LECTURE III

1 *Ulysses: A Critical and Synoptic Edition,* ed. Hans Walter Gabler, with Wolfhard Steppe and Claus Melchior (New York: Garland, 1984).

2 The two principal papers from which Dr Kidd has kindly allowed me to cite the examples given are: ' "Thirteen. Death's Number" Structural Symbolism in *Ulysses',* delivered at the Second Provincetown Joyce Conference, June 1983; and 'Errors of Execution in the 1984 *Ulysses',* delivered to The Society for Textual Scholarship, New York, April 1985. See also his contributions to *The Irish Literary Supplement: A Review of Irish Books* (Fall 1985), pp.41–42.

3 Thomas Hobbes, *Leviathan Or the Matter, Forme, and Power of A Commonwealth Ecclesiasticall and Civil* (1651), part I, chapter 4.

4 In *Focus on 'Citizen Kane'* ed. R. Gottesman (Englewood Cliffs: Prentice-Hall, 1971), pp.127–8.

5 *Image, Music, Text*, p.15.

6 *Focus on 'Citizen Kane'*, p.73. Robert L. Carringer, *The Making of 'Citizen Kane'* (London: John Murray, 1985), should also be consulted; there is a most useful bibliography at pp.165–71.

7 In *The Citizen Kane Book: Comprising The Shooting Script of Citizen Kane by Herman J. Mankiewicz and Orson Welles; The Cutting Continuity Transcript of the Completed Film; preceded by Raising Kane by Pauline Kael* (London: Methuen, 1985), p.83.

8 The British Library Act specifically empowers The British Library to extend its sphere of interest into films and other non-print materials. In a recent position statement prepared for The British Library on non-book materials, Catherine F. Pinion writes: 'It is clear that [non-book materials] represent a major and increasing part of the nation's and the world's output and heritage of recorded knowledge. It is arguable, if not self-evident, that they should receive equivalent treatment to printed material, with regard to collecting, availability, preservation and "bibliographic" control. In actual fact, the position is distinctly inferior in all those respects.' The use of the word 'bibliographic' is inevitable in such a context, but it is to be hoped that its still equivocal status, as signalled by the quotation marks, will be speedily resolved.

9 Perhaps the position is improving. While correcting proof of this text, I purchased (Woolworth, £7.95) a video-cassette of *Citizen Kane*. I have not yet collated it, but am logically committed to do so. The regular note in *TV Times* (paralleled in *The Radio Times*) makes the point: 'Feature films shown on television are not necessarily in the form seen in cinemas. Often several variations are made at the time of production for use according to the intended outlet. In some cases cinema versions may be used, with minor cuts for violence, explicit sex and bad language.'